Coping with complexity:
child and adult poverty

Mark Tomlinson and Robert Walker

CPAG
94 White Lion Street
London N1 9PF

CPAG promotes action for the prevention and relief of poverty among children and families with children. To achieve this, CPAG aims to raise awareness of the causes, extent, nature and impact of poverty, and strategies for its eradication and prevention; bring about positive policy changes for families with children in poverty; and enable those eligible for income maintenance to have access to their full entitlement. If you are not already supporting us, please consider making a donation, or ask for details of our membership schemes, training courses and publications.

Poverty Publication 115

Published by CPAG
94 White Lion Street
London N1 9PF
Tel: 020 7837 7979
staff@cpag.org.uk
www.cpag.org.uk

© Child Poverty Action Group 2009

The views expressed in this book are the authors' and are not necessarily those of CPAG.

A CIP record for this book is available from the British Library

IBSN 978 1 906076 36 8

Cover and design by Devious Designs 0114 275 5634
Typeset by Boldface 020 7833 8868
Printed by Russell Press 0115 978 4505

Child Poverty Action Group is a charity registered in England and Wales (294841) and in Scotland (SC039339), and is a company limited by guarantee, registered in England (1993854).

Acknowledgements

The research on which this book is based was carried out under an ESRC grant (RES-000-23-1418) and we acknowledge the very important contribution made by Glenn Williams of Nottingham Trent University as a co-investigator. We would also like to thank the members of our advisory group for their constructive comments and criticisms throughout the research: Larry Aber (NYU); Kate Green (CPAG); Stephen McKay (University of Birmingham); Mark Shevlin (University of Ulster); and also Dirk Nachbar, Daniel Foster and Amy Morgan of the Department for Work and Pensions. While the merits of the book owe much to all these colleagues, errors, omissions and other inadequacies are ours alone.

Mark Tomlinson
Robert Walker

About the authors

Mark Tomlinson is a Senior Research Officer in the Department of Social Policy and Social Work, University of Oxford, and a Research Associate of Green Templeton College, Oxford. He has worked in several universities as a quantitative social scientist, including Nuffield College Oxford; University of Manchester; National University of Ireland, Galway; Aalborg University, Denmark; and the University of Birmingham. He has published numerous articles in academic journals and books, as well as several reports for institutions such as the OECD, the European Commission, UNIDO, the Department of Trade and Industry, and the Confederation of British Industry. He is currently working on poverty and labour market issues with the aid of a grant from the Joseph Rowntree Foundation.

Robert Walker is a Professor of Social Policy and Fellow of Green Templeton College, University of Oxford. He was formerly Professor of Social Policy at the University of Nottingham and before that Professor of Social Policy Research, Loughborough University where he was Director of the Centre for Research in Social Policy. He is a member of the statutory UK Social Security Advisory Committee and of the Technical Advisory Group, Department of Social Development, South Africa. He chairs the Academic Advisory Committee of the ESRC UK Household Longitudinal Study (Understanding Society) and is a member of the governing board. He is a Research Affiliate of the National Poverty Center, University of Michigan and a Fellow of the Royal Society of Arts. He has published 19 books, 61 research reports and numerous academic articles.

Contents

Preface

On 18 March 2009 it will be the tenth anniversary of Tony Blair's commitment to eradicate child poverty. This ten-year milestone not only gives pause for thought about the difference made to children's lives and life chances by this pledge, but it coincides with a range of challenges and opportunities for tackling poverty. To mark this tenth anniversary, the Child Poverty Action Group will publish two pieces of thought-provoking work around child poverty and wellbeing intended to stimulate debate, and we will publish a manifesto of steps to take anti-poverty policy beyond 2010. This report is the first in this series. As well as coinciding with the tenth anniversary, this innovative work by Mark Tomlinson and Robert Walker is particularly timely.

- The ten-year milestone means we are approaching the target to halve child poverty by 2010/11. *Coping with Complexity* demonstrates that, despite the progress on income poverty, the gap between the policy in place now and what is needed to reach the target is large – Budget 2010 is a vital opportunity to get back on track.
- The Government has announced a commitment to enshrine the 2020 target in law, strengthening the long-term commitment to child poverty eradication, and requiring a strategy and clear reporting on how this goal is being achieved.
- Concerns about unlocking social mobility are rising higher on the policy agenda, with interest being shown from all political quarters and a social mobility White Paper published in January.
- As well as social mobility, concerns about child wellbeing have also been on the increase (triggered by work for UNICEF showing how poorly the UK performs on a range of indicators compared with similar countries). *Coping with Complexity* adds to this by constructing a model of child wellbeing, and comparing it to a model of poverty to understand better some of the causative links between poverty and poor child wellbeing.
- We are moving deeper into recession, with unemployment rapidly climbing. The falling-off of labour demand is a serious risk for families in general and will affect public finances. However, as this report argues, a recession is no excuse for failing to take the measures

needed to tackle poverty, and not to do so would worsen child well-being.

Coping with Complexity sheds light on each of these issues and, in particular, its clear analysis of the interlinked, multi-dimensional nature of poverty in the UK gives a clear steer for how the 2020 legislation ought to be set. Drawing on this research CPAG believes that relative incomes ought to be at the heart of measurement (and reporting) of poverty in the 2020 legislation, but supporting this, a wider set of multi-dimensional features of poverty should also be considered in how policy is constructed. Tomlinson and Walker show not only how important financial strain is to poverty (not identical to income poverty, but linked), but also the limitations of these measures and so the need for a wider approach. Lack of money is at the core of poverty, but other dimensions are also important. Characteristics such as understanding better the physical and social environment, the sigma and psychological strains on families should not replace income measurement, rather these dimensions should contextualise and widen these measures and help condition better policy responses.

The recent clamour of debate around social mobility is tightly focused on children's future chances (for instance, the Government has recently brought in Alan Milburn MP to look at barriers to children from poorer backgrounds joining key professions) and the Government is increasingly linking this to its child poverty commitments. This futures framework is important – one of the most compelling reasons for outrage is the long-term damage poverty does to children, but, as *Coping with Complexity* argues, achieving child wellbeing is much more than this. We should value the quality of childhoods as experienced by children now, not just their future chances of social progression.

Tomlinson and Walker draw from their analysis a series of conclusions about the impact of the recession on adult and child poverty, and in doing so provide food for thought about how the recession should be handled in order to protect children. Two points are worth reiterating. Firstly, expenditure constraints make investment seem harder, but the recession should not delay policies to reduce poverty and improve child wellbeing. Even in the absence of economic growth we must care about the position of our children. Secondly, though protecting jobs is now clearly vital, simply getting people into work does not necessarily lift children out of poverty. Rather, as the authors argue, 'the 'important achievement is not work itself, not even well-paid work, but employment with prospects that leads to longer-term stability'. The welfare reform debate needs to move further on from simply getting people into work, to looking at the quality of employment.

The first ten years of policy to tackle child poverty have led to notable gains. There has been more investment in children, relative income poverty rates have come down (although they rose in 2005/06 and 2006/07), a range of new policy initiatives have been taken and child poverty has been driven to the centre of political debate. We are now at a crossroads, with both the economic crisis threatening this agenda and a series of opportunities to improve policy for children. Mark Tomlinson and Robert Walker's analysis offers clear insights into how these opportunities should be used.

Paul Dornan, Head of Policy, CPAG

Summary

Listening to people talk about their experience of poverty, it is clear that poverty is complex and multi-dimensional. Poverty is more than simply a lack of income. It is the stress caused by the inability to make ends meet, social isolation, and the fatalism and lack of time that prevent political engagement. It is the associated material deprivation, poor housing and neighbourhood. Poverty is a product of multiple causes and can have multifarious, interconnected short- and long-term negative consequences that make life difficult to cope with. Such complexity is easily overlooked and frustrates the best intentions of policymakers who are often tempted to tackle single causes and specific outcomes.

Why multi-dimensional poverty is important

The multi-dimensionality of poverty is evident in the official *Opportunity for All* report, published annually with 41 indicators of poverty. However, this is very different from the realisation that poverty is inherently multi-dimensional, which requires all indices of poverty to be measured for the same individuals so as to capture, insofar as is possible, the multiple complexity of each person's experience of poverty. Some people may score highly on income poverty, but be low on stress and material deprivation. Others will have markedly different profiles across the various dimensions of poverty, arguably experiencing very different kinds of poverty.

The various dimensions of poverty are likely to be causally related, with the possibility that some people may be poor, for example, because they are ill and others ill because they are poor. The direction of causality is important in devising policy responses and in providing individuals with advice, but less so in the measurement of poverty. The challenge for the researcher is to capture the complexity of poverty and for the policy community to take note of its implications for the design and delivery of policy.

Multi-dimensional poverty in Britain

It has hitherto been impossible to develop reliable indicators that adequately capture the complexity of poverty conceived of as a multi-dimensional concept. However, it is now possible by using a statistical technique called 'structural equation modelling'.

The analysis presented here utilises data from the British Household Panel Survey (BHPS), which commenced in 1991 with an initial sample of around 10,000 individuals resident in some 5,000 households. Data limitations required us to limit our analysis to alternate years (1991, 1993, 1995 etc) and to divide our analysis into two parts. The first covered the period 1991 to 2003 and limited the analysis of poverty to four dimensions: financial pressure; psychological strain; social isolation; and civic participation. Improved data allowed a fifth environmental dimension (covering place-based aspects of poverty relating to housing and neighbourhood conditions) to be considered for a later period 1997 to 2003.

In each case, the overall poverty index is most closely related to financial pressure, which is itself a measure that combines financial strain, as indexed by missed housing payments and respondents' own assessment of their financial circumstances, and material deprivation, the lack of ownership of key consumer durables. Financial strain, arguably a measure of short-term or immediate distress, and material deprivation (a more long-term manifestation of poverty) are, in turn, both related directly – though, as others have found, rather weakly – to lack of income. Environment is the dimension next most closely related to the overall index followed by psychological strain, social isolation and civic participation.

The new Poverty Index was fixed in 1991 to ensure that 25 per cent of households were defined as being poor, a proportion similar to the poverty rate indicated by conventional income measures. The poverty rate among some groups proved to be much higher than this, with 58 per cent of lone parents and 39 per cent of single elderly households counting as poor in 1991. Couples with children were no more or less at risk of poverty than the average household. Both the risk and severity of poverty experienced by lone parents is understated if only a measure of low income is used.

Both absolute and relative variants of the Poverty Index (the latter allowing the poverty threshold to vary with average living standards) reveal a steady reduction in poverty between 1991 and 2003. The decline was driven by falls in material deprivation and more especially by reduced financial stress, particularly during the early 1990s, a time when unemployment, inflation and interest rates were all falling. Psychological strain, social isolation and civic participation persisted at similar levels throughout the 13 years, suggesting that financial improvements in people's lives may not immediately negate the exclusionary aspects of poverty.

The dynamics of multi-dimensional poverty

Employment is shown to be a strong defence against poverty, defined in multi-dimensional terms, especially if the work is in a high-status occupation or two or more adults in a household have jobs. However, paid work is not in itself sufficient to sustain a person above the poverty threshold in the long term; it needs to be full-time employment, preferably in a higher status occupation.

Divorce and separation significantly increase the risk of poverty for both partners, but especially for women. Furthermore, the finding that lone parents are still at substantially increased risk of poverty, even after their children have notionally attained financial independence, underlines the long-term consequences of relationship breakdown. Moreover, there is no evidence that re-partnering reduces the risk of poverty or that it is generally possible to 'marry' one's way out of poverty. Only obtaining full-time employment in the highest status occupations can secure a lone parent sustained protection against poverty.

Children's experience of poverty

Children are more likely than adults to live in households that are poor. This is largely because wages are generally set by market rates and take no account of the presence of dependent children. However, the analysis revealed that the child poverty rate fell faster than adult poverty, especially between 2001 and 2003, at which time the Government's policies to reduce child poverty would have been beginning to have an effect. Child poverty measured multi-dimensionally fell faster than income poverty, but poverty associated with parental psychological stress declined only slowly and haphazardly. Lone parents were more likely than other adults to experience psychological stress and parents in couples less so.

Interestingly, children are only rarely found in households experiencing material deprivation, possibly because deprivation is poorly measured. However, the finding underlines the importance parents attach to consumer goods that make servicing children's basic needs more manageable and electronic equipment that can provide entertainment, education or both. These findings illustrate the additional costs associated with bringing up children and the extreme relative deprivation likely to be experienced by the small number of children who live without access to social necessities, such as central heating, a washing machine or a personal computer.

The risk of poverty is highest for children living in households in which the head has a disability or long-term illness, is a lone parent or, like other adults in the household, does not work. Income-based measures appear to exaggerate the importance of worklessness, social housing and household size as factors associated with child poverty compared with the multi-dimensional measure.

Poverty and childhood wellbeing

Poverty affects the wellbeing of children, contributing to low self-worth and increased risky behaviour while detracting from educational orientation and engagement in home life. The strongest negative effect appears to be on home life, followed by that on educational orientation. In contrast, income poverty only has strong detrimental effects on home life and educational orientation.

Financial strain affects all four dimensions of child wellbeing. Poor housing conditions and deprived neighbourhoods are associated with reduced quality of home life, low self-worth and risky behaviour, but material deprivation only increases risky behaviour and negatively affects home life. Children in lone-parent families do less well on all dimensions of wellbeing irrespective of income.

The policy implications of this analysis are direct. Improving home life could be achieved by tackling any dimension of poverty but most effectively by reducing financial pressure. If the goal is to enhance educational performance, then alleviating financial strain and encouraging civic participation of parents may be important strategies since these appear to mediate the effects of poverty on child wellbeing. However, if the aim is to achieve the greatest improvement in wellbeing overall, improving the home and neighbourhood environment is likely to be more effective than reducing material deprivation.

Multi-dimensional poverty and policy

The policy logic that follows from recognition of the true complexity of poverty is both radical and familiar. Within employment policy it is already recognised that a personalised, multi-faceted service is required to assist jobseekers successfully into employment. A similarly holistic policy approach needs to be applied to poverty in which the different dimensions are separately and comprehensively addressed.

It would be understandable, though undoubtedly wrong, to ignore the need for a comprehensive strategy at a time of recession when demands on government are high and expenditure constraints are at their most severe. If job layoffs turn into a deluge of redundancies, the tempta-tion may be to increase conditionality so as to encourage jobseekers to take 'any job', overlooking the findings that only quality jobs offer sus-tained protection against poverty, defined to embrace psychological stress, social isolation and environmental factors as well as financial stress and material deprivation.

A deep recession might also cause government to neglect the impact of separation and divorce on the risk of poverty for the adults and children affected. Children additionally suffer a generalised diminution of wellbeing with lowered self-esteem, poorer home life and an enhanced risk of engaging in risky behaviour. As well as better benefits to reduce the risk and severity of poverty, there is a need for increased support to couples who have recently separated, especially when children are involved.

The analysis also points to the need for a redefinition of the problem of child poverty, focusing more on immediate wellbeing than the dis-advantage as adults. Parental poverty has immediate effects on all aspects of the wellbeing of children. Therefore, any increase in poverty associated with recession is likely to have an instant impact as well as increasing vulnerability to disadvantage later in life. It follows that existing policies to raise family incomes and promote adult employment should be accompanied by a range of new policies, some of which might need to be explicitly child-focused.

Addressing the different dimensions of poverty is likely to have a range of beneficial effects on children. For example, our analysis suggests that implementing a more comprehensive and coherent neighbourhood regeneration policy could improve all aspects of child wellbeing. Furthermore, if such a policy were able to incorporate significant elements of local participation, this might be doubly effective since the analysis found that civic participation by parents had a surprisingly high impact on child wellbeing. The analysis also points to the need to explore ways in which the psychological strain of adults in poor households can be alleviated – as this negatively affects the mental wellbeing of the children, as well as undermining home life.

One

The cause for concern

Poverty has been back on the political agenda for a decade. While Margaret Thatcher, supported by Helmut Kohl in Germany, had successfully banished the word 'poverty' from the political lexicon for a generation, Tony Blair rehabilitated its use in a keynote speech given at Toynbee Hall in March 1999. Blair committed the government to eradicating child poverty, and successfully employed child poverty as a totem in defence of the welfare state and as a clarion cry for welfare reform. As Chancellor, and subsequently as Prime Minister, Gordon Brown has prioritised the child poverty agenda, instigated targets, encouraged non-governmental organisations to build political support and sought to establish mechanisms for departmental collaboration across Whitehall. Under the leadership of David Cameron, the Conservative Party has both embraced the goal to eradicate child poverty and the associated targets, and committed itself to addressing the causes of poverty. While there may not be political – or indeed research – consensus as to the 'real' causes of poverty, there has been a determined effort to address the problem, which looks like continuing whatever the political complexion of government.

The political momentum to tackle poverty and to eradicate child poverty has had important results. The risk of a child being in poverty – defined as less than 60 per cent of the median equivalised household income before housing costs – fell from 27 per cent in 1997/98 to 21 per cent in 2004/05, the equivalent of almost 700,000 children being lifted out of poverty.[1] When child poverty is measured against a standard held constant in real terms, it more than halved – from 28 per cent to 13 per cent. During the same period, the proportion of pensioners in relative poverty fell more slowly, from 25 per cent to 21 per cent, while the overall poverty rate declined from 20 per cent to 17 per cent.

However, in the next two years, 2005/06 and 2006/07, child poverty rose again by a total of between 100,000 and 200,000, and the overall poverty rate increased from 17 per cent to 18 per cent. Moreover, while the risk of poverty for children living in households where neither parent is working is very high indeed – 68 per cent – a reflection of the low level of welfare benefits, finding a job is no guarantee of affluence. One in five chil-

Figure 1.1

Trends in poverty, 1994/05 to 2006/07

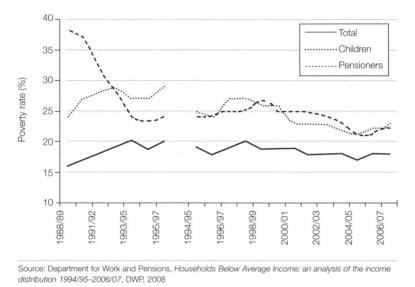

Source: Department for Work and Pensions, *Households Below Average Income: an analysis of the income distribution 1994/95–2006/07*, DWP, 2008

dren (20 per cent) in households where one parent works full time and the other stays at home remain in poverty. Only when both parents work – one full time and the other part time – or when a lone parent is employed full time does the risk of poverty faced by a child (3 per cent and 7 per cent respectively) fall below that of an average person. Given that the Government had hoped to lift 25 per cent of children out of poverty by 2005/06 and achieved a 21 per cent reduction, the goal of a 50 per cent reduction by 2010/11 now appears to be immensely challenging.

It is true that a number of important policy changes have been made that would not have had a chance to show up in the figures cited above. These include increases in the level of the child element of child tax credit and in child benefit for the first child and the disregarding of child benefit in calculating income used to means-test housing benefit. The Government calculates that planned extra expenditure of about £2 billion will take about 500,000 children out of poverty, about half the number required to reach the 2010/11 target.[2] There is clearly a need to reinvigorate policies to eradicate child poverty and substantially to reduce the level of poverty experienced by other groups.

Recognising the reality of poverty

Disappointing though the results of anti-poverty measures have proved to be, few policy makers ever expected that the task of eradicating poverty would be an easy one. To illustrate this, the Child Poverty Action Group (CPAG) has been in existence since 1965. It is widely regarded as one of the most effective political lobbying organisations in Britain, not least because its campaigns are underpinned by empirical research and sophisticated policy analysis. Its intellectual credibility and policy sophistication means that it has remained influential irrespective of the party in power. Nevertheless, the telling fact is that poverty has risen more than it has fallen during the four decades of CPAG's existence.

The research conducted by CPAG and others helps to illustrate the challenges confronting policy makers. Poverty is a complex phenomenon. Most obviously, poverty refers to the lack of resources required to meet the basic needs of individuals living in a family or household. However, basic needs are likely to change over time as the economy grows, living standards rise, and the expectations and demands created by society alter. This means that poverty cannot simply be eradicated by the economic growth delivered by a successful economy, since greater wealth serves to increase the threshold distinguishing poor people from all others. Instead, it is necessary to redistribute resources between the two groups, meaning that a more affluent portion of the population will need to forgo income, or increases in income, in order to lift others out of poverty. For this reason, and others to do with differing attitudes and ideology, basic needs are themselves contested, making it difficult to build political support for tackling poverty.[3] Nevertheless, as an important prerequisite for creating popular backing for anti-poverty policies, the Joseph Rowntree Foundation has demonstrated that it is possible for laypeople to reach a consensus about the standard of living that families need to enjoy if they are to avoid poverty.[4]

Poverty is more than simply a lack of income. It is equally the stress caused by a family's inability to make ends meet. It is the poor housing or homelessness, the lack of facilities, infrastructure and stimulation, the fear of crime and the possible lack of respect resulting from living in a deprived area. It is the inability to acquire or renew possessions and the reduced opportunities to fulfil personal ambitions or to exploit opportunities in employment, sport, education, the arts and/or in the local neighbourhood. It is the lack of personal contacts, sometimes arising from the inability to reciprocate, the perceived futility of political engagement and the poor physical and mental health, itself a product of bad living conditions, day-to-day pressure and debilitating personal circumstances.

This multi-dimensionality of poverty is now recognised by the Government. Each year it publishes the *Opportunity for All* report, which includes 41 different indicators of poverty.[5] The New Policy Institute annually publishes an additional set of 50 indicators.[6] However, one problem with this plethora of indicators is that it can lead to a vacuous debate as government spotlights measures that show improvement and critics focus on indicators that have worsened, thereby dissipating public attention and polarising political discussion.

Another problem with multiple indicators, one that is exacerbated when indicators are framed as targets, is that policy is devised to maximise the impact on one aspect of poverty to the possible detriment of others. To the extent that poverty is truly multi-faceted with the various dimensions being interactive, cumulative or both, targeted policies are likely to be minimally effective on the problem as a whole, equivalent to sticking an elastoplast on a malignant rash.

Poverty is caused by many factors and has many, often negative, effects. Some babies are born into poverty and, less frequently, spend their entire childhoods in poverty, with the consequence that the statistical likelihood that they will grow up to be poor in adulthood is much increased.[7] Some people become poor in early adulthood if they have limited skills, are in poor health or have children before they are able to establish a secure foothold in the labour market. Others may become poor later in life because of a plethora of reasons that affect them directly or indirectly including accident, ill health, pregnancy and childbirth, relationship breakdown, unemployment and redundancy. Some will remain poor; others, albeit a small proportion, will go on to enjoy a life of affluence. Most will carry forward the scars of poverty; once poor, the probability of becoming poor again rises noticeably. Poor children achieve lower exam results,[8] experience more poor physical and mental health as children and adults,[9] are more likely to be affected by and to engage in crime[10] and to experience worklessness as adults than their non-poor contemporaries.[11] Adults with intermittent work histories and low pay have a high risk of being poor in old age, not least because the social security and pension systems tend to map the inequalities experienced in work onto retirement.

Poverty is further complicated by the rapidity of social change and by fluctuations in individual circumstances. Not long ago, policy debates contrasted the poor with the non-poor as if the two groups never changed places. In fact, there is a great deal of 'churning', with more than half of Britons having had an annual income below the poverty threshold at least once in the last decade. The majority of spells of poverty are short-lived. However, most poor people experience more than one spell of poverty and some people remain poor for long periods: 17 per cent of children were poor in three of the four years between 2002 and 2005 as were 13 per cent of pensioners.[12] Policy rarely discriminates between the different kinds of poverty – transient, occasional, recurrent, chronic and permanent – and yet there is evidence, albeit mostly from abroad, that different social groups are differentially prone to the various kinds of poverty with diverse short- and long-term consequences.

Poverty, then, is a multi-faceted phenomenon of considerable complexity. The product of multiple causes, it often has multifarious negative consequences that make life hard to live and sometimes very difficult to cope with. Its effects are both short and long term. In a world of sound bites, such complexity is easily overlooked.

Responding to the complexity of poverty

The failure of the Government to stay on track towards eradicating poverty is explicable in many ways: hesitant political leadership in the context of limited popular support; excessive concern about the hostility of the median voter; unanticipated events, notably 9/11, 11/7 and Iraq; political expediency and the failure to align benefit rates with poverty thresholds; and, more recently, the collapse of confidence in the global economy. Less self-evident, although still of considerable importance, has been the collective failure adequately to confront the inherent complexity of poverty, both its nature and causality.

Modern politics, driven as it is by media interest and short attention spans, cannot easily accommodate nuance and difference. Likewise, policies to be delivered nationally by a variety of government, private and voluntary organisations favour simplified bureaucratic solutions that can be readily communicated, easily computerised and straightforwardly audited. Nevertheless, if policy is to be effective, there is a need to recognise that the diversity in the causes and effects of poverty calls for differentiated policy responses. The commitment to personalised and tailored services provided by Jobcentre Plus reflects a comparatively new appreciation of this need. However, the precise pattern of causality is not well understood in relation to the many dimensions of disadvantage that define the experience of poverty. Do, for example, poor people living in deprived neighbourhoods suffer more than low-income families in affluent neighbourhoods, and is it better to target policies on poor areas or poor families?[13] Even the seemingly simple question of whether tenants in social housing are income poor because they are social tenants or social tenants because they are income poor is contested with quite bizarre policy implications.[14]

Likewise, the diversity in the nature and experience of poverty requires the sensitive application of a greater range of policy interventions, while an understanding of the temporal characteristics of poverty may help in achieving this through improved targeting. The occurrence of events that can precipitate poverty is far greater than the number of people who experience poverty as a consequence.[15] There is potential, therefore, to identify factors that mediate the negative consequences of events and to extend protection to those who would otherwise be more exposed. Similarly, people who have experienced one spell of poverty are measurably more at risk of experiencing poverty again and could be targeted with preventative interventions. Furthermore, if the type of poverty in terms of its severity or likely duration could be assessed at onset, then tailored support could again be offered.

It is in this context, therefore, that the research reported in this book seeks to explore the complexity of the phenomenon of poverty not, as academics are sometimes wont to do, simply for its own sake, but rather to exploit an understanding of the complexity to inform the design of better, more effective policy. Underpinning this investigation is a set of novel statistical techniques, generally referred to as 'structural equation modelling', that allow us to handle the complexities of real life more efficiently than has hitherto been possible. However, for the most part we focus on the findings and the lessons rather than the methodology that makes this novel investigation possible.

The remainder of the book is organised as follows. The multidimensional nature of poverty is first explored in **Chapter 2** and then, in **Chapter 3**, the extent of multi-dimensional poverty in Britain is mapped out and its development plotted throughout the 1990s and early 2000s. In **Chapter 4**, attention shifts to the dynamics of multi-dimensional poverty and to two questions in particular: can poverty trajectories be predicted and what could be done to prevent the continuation of repeated spells of poverty. In **Chapter 5**, we discuss the overall state and prevalence of child poverty in the UK, while **Chapter 6** examines the consequences of family poverty for the wellbeing of children and young people, not in the future when they reach adulthood, but in the here and now. It shows that various dimensions of family poverty affect children in different ways and that distinctive policy measures are required to stem the negative consequences of poverty. Finally, in **Chapter 7** we return to consider in more detail the policy implications for tackling poverty.

Notes

1   Department for Work and Pensions, *Households Below Average Income: an analysis of the income distribution 1994/95–2006/07*, Department for Work and Pensions, 2008

2   Joseph Rowntree Foundation, *Child Poverty Updates, June 2008: progress since 2006*, Joseph Rowntree Foundation, 2008, available at www.jrf.org.uk/child-poverty/updates.asp (accessed 11 September 2008)

3   M Orton and K Rowlingson, *Public Attitudes to Economic Inequality*, Joseph Rowntree Foundation, 2007

4   J Bradshaw and others, *Minimum Income Standards in Britain*, Joseph Rowntree Foundation, 2008

5   Department for Work and Pensions, *Opportunity for All: indicators update 2007*, Department for Work and Pensions, 2008, available at www.dwp.gov.uk/ofa/reports/2007/OpportunityforAll2007.pdf (accessed 11 September 2008)

6   G Palmer, T MacInnes and P Kenway, *Monitoring Poverty and Social Exclusion 2007*, New Policy Institute, 2007, available at www.poverty.org.uk/reports/mpse%202007.pdf (accessed 11 September 2008)

7   J Hobcraft, *Continuity and Change in Pathways to Young Adult Disadvantage: results from a British birth cohort*, CASE Paper 66, Centre for Analysis of Social Exclusion, London School of Economics, 2003

8   National Statistics, *National Curriculum Assessment, GCSE and Equivalent Attainment and Post-16 Attainment by Pupil Characteristics in England, 2006/07*, Department for Children, Schools and Families, 2007

9   HM Treasury, *Ending Child Poverty: everybody's business*, HM Treasury, 2008, available at www.hm-treasury.gov.uk/media/d/bud08_childpoverty_1310.pdf (accessed 11 September 2008)

10 J Neale, 'Children, Crime and Illegal Drug Use', in J Bradshaw and E Mayhew (eds), *The Well-being of Children in the UK*, Save the Children, 2005

11 J Griggs with R Walker, *The Costs of Child Poverty for Individuals and Society: a literature review*, Joseph Rowntree Foundation, 2008

12 Department for Work and Pensions, *Households Below Average Income: an analysis of the income distribution 1994/95–2006/07*, Department for Work and Pensions, 2008, p169

13 J Griggs, A Whitworth, R Walker, D McLennan and M Noble, *Person or Place-based Policies to Tackle Disadvantage? Not knowing what works*, Joseph Rowntree Foundation, 2008

14 For example, the then newly appointed former housing minister Caroline Flint questioned 'whether it would be right to ask new tenants who can work to sign 'commitment contracts' when getting a tenancy, agreeing to engage with job-seeking or training in return for better support', *New Statesman*, 12 February 2008

15 R Walker, 'Opportunity and Life Chances: the dynamics of poverty, inequality and exclusion', in P Diamond and A Giddens (eds), *The New Egalitarianism*, Polity Press, 2005, pp69-85

Two
Why multi-dimensional poverty is important

For a not insignificant number of people the problem of poverty in Britain is a no-brainer; there simply is none.

This view, that poverty has been extinguished by economic and social progress, was one espoused by Margaret Thatcher across the capitals of Europe and it did her little political harm at home. Often people who hold to this position understand poverty to be a near-death state of abject hunger and distress, epitomised by 'images of malnourished 'third-world' children, or if pressed to consider the British context, a bygone age of Dickensian squalor'.[1] Opinion polls typically suggest that around 40 per cent of people believe that there is very little poverty in Britain today.[2]

In most surveys, however, people who believe poverty is a problem that has largely been consigned to history are outnumbered by the small majority of Britons who would argue that there is 'quite a lot of poverty in Britain today'. This discrepancy of view does not seem to be one that is shaped by either knowledge or experience. Rather, it appears to reflect differences in deep-seated values. Some people consider that poverty results from indolence exacerbated by high benefits and profligate public expenditure. Overwhelmingly this group tends to adhere to a strict definition of poverty ('someone cannot eat and live without getting into debt') and thereby to conclude that poverty is no longer a problem in Britain. In contrast, people who believe that poverty is the product of unfairness and social injustice, low benefits and insufficient government action are much more prepared to countenance a definition of poverty that refers to a person's inability to buy 'things that others take for granted' and therefore to accept that poverty continues to be a scourge in Britain. It is hardly surprising, therefore, that it has proved so difficult to build a popular consensus to invest in eradicating poverty.

Moreover, very few people admit to being poor. Rather they use terms such as struggling, money being tight, being hard up or having a hard time to describe their circumstances. This failure to self-diagnose poverty may reflect the sense of shame that attaches to poverty. This is externally reinforced by stigmatising language and procedures encountered when dealing with public agencies, and by the attitudes and expectations of the public at large. Moreover, the fact that most people in poverty see themselves as coping well in adverse circumstances and being better off than many others does not accord with the popular notion of poverty as penury and the result of moral failings and budgeting incompetence.

What people on low incomes report is a situation of great complexity in which the pressures they face are cumulative.[3] Basics become luxuries that have to be prioritised and saved for. Solutions to one problem create problems of their own, as when saving on heating exacerbates illness and borrowing from the rent money generates arrears and threats of eviction. Poverty feels like entrapment when options are always lacking, the future is looming and unpredictable and guilt seems ever present, arising from an inability to meet one's children's needs, one's own expectations and society's demands.

That large numbers of people confront the problems of poverty daily is indisputable, despite being seemingly invisible to a large minority of their fellow citizens. What is also the case is that the complexity of poverty and the experience of poverty is seldom given adequate attention in policy debates, be it in discussions of the measurement of poverty or in the design and implementation of policies to combat it. This book seeks to rectify this omission and to place the complex experience of poverty at the heart of the analysis in the hope that this will lead to the prospect of more effective policy. To this end, in this chapter, we explain the reasons why debates about poverty have come to be oversimplified before setting out the case for viewing poverty multi-dimensionally.

The early days of measurement

The early pioneers who researched poverty, Henry Mayhew,[4] Charles Booth[5] and Seebohm Rowntree,[6] all grappled with its complexity. Rowntree notably distinguished between different categories of poverty and recognised the need to take account of social conditions, diet and health as well as income in assessing living standards. However, in the nineteenth century, for those who looked, poverty was self-evident, with large numbers existing in squalor, without sufficient food, decent clothing or adequate heating or sanitation. The pioneers' interest in measuring poverty was moral and instrumental rather than scientific; they wanted to mobilise political support so as to ameliorate the conditions of the poor. Moreover, this goal demanded that they show that poverty was due to a lack of resources rather than to profligate spending. Hence, these pioneers paid considerable attention to establishing how much income their poor respondents had, as well as how much it cost to provide for the basic necessities of life.

The focus on income proved enduring, partly because income is comparatively easy to measure – or would seem to be. It provides the basis for the United Nations' Millennium Development Goals – income less than one or two dollars a day – and constitutes the core component of the UK child poverty target – household income less than 60 per cent of the median. However, the apparent simplicity of measurement is largely illusory. Income is typically under-reported in surveys, partly because people often mistakenly equate income with earnings and/or with cash thereby omitting sources such as interest payments and income in kind. Income fluctuates much more than consumption, meaning that income-based measures suggest that living standards oscillate much more than they probably do. It is also difficult to know how income is allocated within families, to children for example, and how far this equates with needs.

More important however, it might be argued that income is merely an indirect measure of poverty, since poverty is really experienced as the inability to consume at a level that would enable someone to engage in a normal way of life. Ringen takes this view, noting that true poverty is manifest as deprivation, 'visible poverty', self-evident to those who look.[7] Moreover, he argues that low income and deprivation are intrinsically different and can lead to contrasting policy responses. Whereas income poverty could be eradicated by ensuring that poor people are given the precise amount of additional income to lift them above the poverty line, such additional income would not guarantee reduced deprivation.

Poverty in the here and now

People who deny that poverty exists in Britain tend to take an absolutist view of poverty; that it is a matter of life and death. US commentators on the British scene, such as Charles Murray, are apt to take a similar view, not least because the US poverty standard is fixed as a multiple of money needed for food and is only uprated in line with prices.[8] In Britain, even at the turn of the twentieth century, Rowntree was aware of the necessity to take account of needs beyond mere subsistence.[9]

Coinciding with the foundation of CPAG, Brian Abel-Smith and Peter Townsend recognised that the basic necessities were changing as the austerity of earlier years gave way to growing affluence for an increasing number of people.[10] They also appreciated that, simultaneously, a lack of income was preventing some people from engaging in the activities and expenditure expected of them, causing them to be excluded and stigmatised. They argued eloquently for a relative definition of poverty and introduced one in their book, *The Poor and the Poorest*. This set various income thresholds that were expressed as different percentages above the prevailing rate of means-tested benefits (then called national assistance) and which indicated varying degrees of hardship.[11]

Subsequently, measures of relative poverty have been refined, with thresholds set as a proportion of median equivalent household income. Equivalent income is income that is adjusted in an attempt to take account of differences in household size and composition, and the varying needs of adults and children. Median income is used as a reference point, rather than the mean (the simple average), because it is less affected by the incomes of the comparatively small number of extremely rich households. While in some respects these measures are an improvement on Brian Abel-Smith and Peter Townsend's index, they have certain defects. First, because they are not tied to benefit levels they do not provide a direct measure of the effectiveness of policy; in the US some benefit rates are set relative to the poverty line but British governments have never explicitly set benefits to be at or above the poverty line. Secondly, the measures relate to income poverty which, as already noted, provides only a partial, and arguably biased, measure of true poverty. Thirdly, and for associated reasons, relative income measures can sometimes generate perverse results. Income inequalities often tend to increase during periods of high economic growth (which increases median income and hence the associated poverty thresholds) at a faster rate than incomes rise overall. As a consequence, at times when almost everybody, including low-income families, is getting richer, the observed poverty rate will actually rise, while the reverse can be true during economic recessions. Furthermore, when the economy is growing, poor households are likely to experience some improvement in their absolute living standards, in the number or quality of products or services that they purchase, which will go unrecorded in statistics measuring relative poverty. The Government therefore now produces a series of poverty statistics in which the poverty line is held constant in real terms.[12]

Peter Townsend was aware of the partial nature of income measures, later arguing that poverty was not the lack of income necessary to purchase a basket of goods, but rather the lack of resources required to participate fully in society.[13] He compiled a list of common items and activities and showed that many people on low incomes went without them, although he was criticised for his 'arbitrary' selection of indicators and for presuming that people who lacked items were invariably deprived by lack of income rather than through the exercise of choice and personal preference. Subsequently, many studies of deprivation have avoided the problem of 'deprivation through choice' by explicitly asking respondents whether or not they lacked possessions or failed to engage in activities because of a shortage of income.[14] The possessions and activities selected as indicators are now often chosen because a majority of the population considers them to be 'social necessities' that 'nobody should have to do without'.[15] Such 'majoritarian' or 'consensual' measures are inherently relative.

Studies that compare material deprivation and income poverty show them to be only moderately correlated. Calandrino, for example, finds 32 per cent of British lone parents to be both poor and multiply deprived and another 36 per cent to be either poor or deprived.[16] Such findings lend support to Ringen's contention that the two concepts are distinct and should be differentiated although the lack of association might simply be the result of measurement error.[17] The differences between income poverty and deprivation could also be a product of the ways that families cope in times of adversity. There are likely to be time lags between a drop in income and the depreciation or sale of assets that might follow. Indeed, asset sales might precede a drop of income if families adopted the strategy to prepare for harder times. Whatever the reason, differences between income poverty and deprivation point to the need simultaneously to measure and report both, a strategy that has now been adopted by the Government. This approach has the further advantage that deprivation measures are less affected by the perverse effects of economic growth and changes in income inequality.

For many years, Britain did not have an official poverty standard, although by convention a relative income measure was adopted with the threshold set at household income below 60 per cent of the median. Since 2003, this measure has been taken by the Government as one of three used to monitor progress towards the eradication of child poverty.[18] The second is an absolute measure – the 60 per cent threshold fixed at the 1998/99 level – and the third is a composite measure, counting the numbers who are both materially deprived and have an income below 70 per cent of contemporary median equivalised household income. These three measures are intended to be supported by other multi-dimensional indicators included in the annual *Opportunity for All* publication.

It would be churlish not to acknowledge the progress made in the official measurement of poverty and wrong to deny a political commitment to tackle the problem. Nevertheless, the measures currently employed fall far short of capturing the multi-dimensional experience of poverty described above.

Multi-dimensional poverty

Poverty is not just the absence of income or even the material deprivation that accompanies it. It is both of these and everything that follows from them: the hassle; the stress; the hard work; the budgeting; the conflict; the shame; the degraded environment; the isolation; the helplessness; the ill health; the misfortune – and much else that, taken together, is both a reasoned and involuntary response to hardship and which may, quite often, serve to exacerbate it.

Social exclusion first entered the British political vocabulary in the 1980s when European governments insisted on continuing debates about poverty in opposition to Margaret Thatcher and Helmut Kohl. Social exclusion became a euphemism for poverty. With the creation of the defunct Social Exclusion Unit (now the Social Exclusion Task Force) in 1997, social exclusion was re-interpreted 'to be more than income poverty':

> It is a shorthand term for what can happen when people or areas have a combination of linked problems, such as unemployment, discrimination, poor skills, low incomes, poor housing, high crime and family breakdown. These problems are linked and mutually reinforcing. Social exclusion is an extreme consequence of what happens when people don't get a fair deal throughout their lives, often because of disadvantage they face at birth, and this disadvantage can be transmitted from one generation to the next.[19]

This shorthand emphasises the multi-dimensionality of social exclusion, the reinforcing nature of the various forms of disadvantage and its extreme consequences. Leaving aside, for the moment, the fact that the Task Force applies the concept of social exclusion to areas as well as individuals, social exclusion could equally be characterised as severe poverty. Whereas poverty is traditionally thought of as a state, with poor people contrasted with the non-poor, and all poor people assumed to be pretty much the same, it might be more accurate to view poverty as a matter of degree. The same reinforcing dimensions of disadvantage apply to all people in poverty but to a different degree. In terms of measurement, each poor person would have a set of scores, one for each dimension, with the degree of poverty indicated by the accumulated scores. (The same dimensions could equally be applied to the non-poor as, indeed, they are in Chapter 3.) People's scores on the various dimensions are likely to change over time, not least because of the reinforcing nature of disadvantage. Social and psychological supports that protect people, good physical and mental health, social capital and competence, and civic engagement, can all be casualties of low income and may, in certain circumstances, be compounded if mediated by the negative characteristics of poor places, such as dilapidated infrastructure, isolation, crime and redlining. This can result in people being caught in a destructive social and economic down-current, although, equally, there is considerable evidence of poor people resisting such forces through a mixture of their own agency, appropriate support and good fortune.[20]

What are the dimensions of disadvantage that comprise poverty? Clearly the accoutrements, or lack of them, that would enable Ringen to identify visible poverty. These would include: housing and housing quality; fuel and warmth; clothing (the amount, its quality and whether fashionable or otherwise); material deprivation (defined quite broadly to include furniture, soft furnishings, white goods and electronics including those used for entertainment); and access to transport. Such commodities, to exploit the language and ideas of Amartya Sen, enable people to function adequately in society and, in Britain, are largely acquired through spending and hence are dependent on income and savings, which would ideally be separately measured.[21] To these commodities, one could add others that would help a person function economically – for example, access to credit, insurance and childcare.

A dimension often neglected in policy debates, but which looms large in the experience of poor people, is the stress associated with poverty. This manifests itself in many ways. It is the constant prioritising and juggling; the anxiety; the fighting of the structure and seeming inflexibility of the benefits system; the conflict with officialdom and with partners; the inability to say 'yes' to a child who refuses to take 'no' for an answer; the lack of space and time; the absence of satisfaction; the humiliation, low esteem and sense of helplessness. It is perhaps possible to distinguish between the direct financial stress or distress of debt and going without and its emotional consequences. Indeed, Sen argues, that while poverty is relative, differing according to context, poverty experienced as shame is absolute, everywhere the same, arising from people's inability fully to function as members of their community.[22]

Closely related to the dimension of shame is that of health. Many studies have shown physical and mental ill health to be either a cause or a consequence of income poverty.[23] So close and so ubiquitous is the relationship that it is sensible always to register the health of a person with low income. Clearly, the affluent are not immune to poor health, but poor people seldom fully escape it.[24]

Similarly associated with stress is the social isolation frequently reported as a manifestation or consequence of poverty and which itself can be a risk factor associated with downward spirals into social exclusion. Not only does it typically cost money to engage in the reciprocity that helps support social networks, it requires confidence and emotional energy that can be drained by living on a tight budget.[25] Once marginalised, the effect becomes self-reinforcing, leaving the person with few contacts to whom to turn for practical, financial or emotional support. There is considerable evidence too that poor people often have limited social capital with few links that bridge social domains, and are either frequently excluded, or frequently exclude themselves, from civic participation. Not surprisingly, complex relationships are also found between poverty, social networks and health.[26]

As noted above, the Social Exclusion Task Force applies the concept of social exclusion to geographic areas as well as to people, implying that some localities are social excluded and, perhaps, also, that some are socially excluding. Obviously it is true that all people live in places, contribute to places and are affected by places. Moreover, it is probable that poverty and disadvantage are mediated by place and places affected by the poverty or otherwise of their inhabitants. However, the associations are likely to be complex. The fact that poverty is concentrated in areas of social housing might be, as is a current ministerial concern, attributable to localised 'cultures of worklessness' but could equally be a consequence of policies to house people with priority needs, many of whom will also face substantial barriers to employment. Spatial concentrations of low-income families may or may not be characterised by dense, supportive networks, but are unlikely to provide social capital that fosters rapid upward social mobility. Such areas are unlikely to be well endowed with good schools, accessible cultural facilities and generously funded public services but, equally, the poor person living in more affluent areas may have less access to affordable facilities and be inhibited in building local networks. However, whatever the precise circumstances, it is rational to assume that a person's experience of poverty is likely to be partly shaped by the characteristics of the neighbourhood in which s/he lives. Place is itself a further dimension of the personal phenomenon of poverty.

Causes and dimensions

Listening to poor people talk, it is clear that multi-dimensionality is inherent in poverty and the experience of poverty. A person who lacks income is likely also to live in inadequate housing, perhaps in a bad area, to be in debt, and to feel stressed, isolated and personally inadequate. It will not always be the case; as in all things, it is a matter of degree.

It is important to recognise that the concept of multi-dimensional poverty introduced in this chapter is very different from the multiple measures available in the Government's annual *Opportunity for All* report. The 41 *Opportunity for All* indices cover different aspects of poverty and relate to different individuals; there is some overlap between individuals counted as income poor and those who are recorded as being materially deprived, but it is incomplete. In contrast, the multi-dimensionality considered here relates to the same individuals, the aim being to capture, insofar as is possible, the multiple complexity of each person's experience of poverty. Some people may score highly on income poverty, but be low on stress and material deprivation. Others will have very different profiles across the various dimensions of poverty, arguably experiencing very different kinds of poverty.

The various dimensions of poverty are likely to be inherently causally related and there will always be debate about the direction of causality. Is someone poor because they are ill, or ill because they are poor? Are they in debt because they have too little money or lack money because they are in debt? Such questions are important. The direction of causality is relevant at the individual level for, to take one example, the debt adviser dealing with a client. It is also of concern at a strategic policy level. Building political support for anti-poverty programmes is easier when the majority of the poor are demonstrably more sinned against than sinning. Knowledge of the direction of causality might also help in prioritising resources, say, between healthcare and social security.

Table 2.1

Official measure of material deprivation

The survey question

Do you and your family have…

Are you and your family able to afford to…

Possible responses:

[1] 'We have this'

[2] 'We would like to have this, but cannot afford it at the moment'

[3] 'We do not want/need this at the moment'

Adult deprivation	Child deprivation
Keep your home adequately warm	A holiday away from home at least one week a year with his or her family
Two pairs of all-weather shoes for each adult	
Enough money to keep your home in a decent state of repair	Swimming at least once a month
	A hobby or leisure activity
A holiday away from home for one week a year, not staying with relatives	Friends round for tea or a snack once a fortnight
Replace any worn-out furniture	Enough bedrooms for every child over 10 of different sex to have her/his own bedroom
A small amount of money to spend each week on yourself, not on your family	Leisure equipment (for example, sports equipment or a bicycle)
Regular savings (of £10 a month) for rainy days or retirement	Celebrations on special occasions, such as birthdays, Christmas or other religious festivals
Insurance of contents of dwelling	
Have friends or family for a drink or meal at least once a month	Play group/nursery/toddler group at least once a week for children of pre-school age
A hobby or leisure activity	Going on a school trip at least once a term for school-aged children
Replace or repair broken electrical goods such as refrigerator or washing machine	

Source: Department for Work and Pensions, *Measuring Child Poverty*, DWP, 2003, p21

However, causality need not be an issue when it comes to the measurement of poverty. It does not much matter to a poor person today whether s/he is in debt because s/he is in poor housing or in poor housing because of the debt: the person is both in debt and in poor housing, neither is pleasant and experiencing both is undoubtedly worse than either just being in debt or living in poor housing without the additional burden of debt. Over time, the level of a person's debt and the quality of housing may change and the degree of improvement or deterioration in each may measurably affect the nature of the poverty experienced. Again, from the perspective of measuring poverty, it is irrelevant whether the level of debt and the quality of housing are related, although, of course, the people themselves may seek a trade-off between the level of debt they incur and the quality of housing they enjoy (or suffer).

Poverty, then, is complex, inherently multi-dimensional, but real. The challenge for the researcher is to capture the complexity of this reality and for the policy community to take note of its implications for the design and delivery of policy.

Notes

1 S Castell and J Thompson, *Understanding Attitudes to Poverty in the UK: getting the public's attention*, Joseph Rowntree Foundation, 2007, p10

2 A Park, M Phillips and C Robinson, *Attitudes to Poverty: findings from the British Social Attitudes Survey*, Joseph Rowntree Foundation, 2007

3 C-A Hooper, S Gorin, C Cabral and C Dyson, *Living with Hardship 24/7: the diverse experiences of families in poverty in England*, The Frank Buttle Trust, 2007

4 H Mayhew, *London Labour and London Poor*, Griffin, Bohn and Company, 1851

5 C Booth, *Life and Labour of the People in London (1889–1903)*, Macmillan, 1892

6 S Rowntree, *Poverty: a study of town life*, Macmillan, 1901

7 S Ringen, 'Direct and Indirect Measures of Poverty', *Journal of Social Policy* 17(3),1988, pp351-65

8 R Blank, 'How to Improve Poverty Measurement in the United States', *Journal of Policy Analysis and Management* 27(2), 2008, pp233-54

9 J Veit-Wilson, 'Paradigms of Poverty: a rehabilitation of JS Rowntree', *Journal of Social Policy* 15, 1986

10 B Abel-Smith and P Townsend, *The Poor and the Poorest*, Bell, 1965

11 B Abel-Smith and P Townsend, *The Poor and the Poorest*, Bell, 1965

12 Department for Work and Pensions, *Households Below Average Income: an analysis of the income distribution 1994/95–2006/07*, Department for Work and Pensions, 2008

13 P Townsend, *Poverty in the United Kingdom*, Allen Lane, 1979

14 R Berthoud, M Bryan and E Bardasi, *The Relationship Between Income and Material Deprivation over Time*, DWP Research Report 219, Corporate Document Services, 2004; D Gordon and others, *Poverty and Social Exclusion in Britain*, Joseph Rowntree Foundation, 2000

15 D Gordon and others, *Poverty and Social Exclusion in Britain*, Joseph Rowntree Foundation, 2000

16 M Calandrino, *Low Income and Deprivation in British Families*, DWP Working Paper 10, Department for Work and Pensions, 2003

17 R Berthoud, M Bryan and E Bardasi, *The Relationship Between Income and Material Deprivation over Time*, DWP Research Report 219, Corporate Document Services, 2004

18 Department for Work and Pensions, *Measuring Child Poverty*, Department for Work and Pensions, 2003

19 Social Fund Task Force, available at www.cabinetoffice.gov.uk/social_exclusion _task_force/context.aspx (accessed 12 September 2008)

20 C-A Hooper, S Gorin, C Cabral and C Dyson, *Living with Hardship 24/7: the diverse experiences of families in poverty in England*, The Frank Buttle Trust, 2007; E Kempson, *Life on a Low Income*, York Publishing Services, 1996

21 A Sen, *Commodities and Capabilities*, Oxford University Press,1999

22 A Sen, 'Poor, Relatively Speaking', *Oxford Economic Papers* 35(2), 1983, pp153-69

23 S Payne, 'Mental Health, Poverty and Social Exclusion', in C Pantazis, D Gordon and R Levitas (eds), *Poverty and Social Exclusion in Britain: the Millennium survey*, The Policy Press, 2006

24 S Weich and G Lewis, 'Poverty, Unemployment and Common Mental Disorders: population-based cohort study', *British Medical Journal* 317, 1998, pp115–19

25 D Gallie, S Paugam and S Jacobs, 'Unemployment, Poverty and Social Isolation: is there a vicious circle of social exclusion?' *European Societies* 5(1), 2003, pp1-32

26 V Cattell, 'Poor People, Poor Places and Poor Health: the mediating role of social networks and social capital', *Social Science and Medicine* 52, 2001, pp1501-16

Three

Multi-dimensional poverty in Britain

It is easy to agree that poverty is complex and multi-dimensional but, until very recently, it has not been possible to develop reliable indicators that adequately capture the complexity and which are sufficiently stable for trends in poverty rates to be identified. In this chapter, we briefly explain how we measure multi-dimensional poverty before reporting results that recast our understanding of the nature and distribution of poverty in Britain.

Measuring poverty as a multi-dimensional concept

A useful starting point when it comes to measuring poverty is Ringen's recognition of the measurement assumption and the income assumption that underpin much poverty research. The former refers to the belief that poverty exists and as such can be measured; while this assumption is widely contested, it is self-evidently necessary given the task at hand. The latter assumption asserts that poverty can be measured in terms of a deficit in income in relation to needs, a presumption that – as we have seen – becomes increasingly untenable if poverty is defined as the complex multi-dimensional phenomenon described above. Baulch has usefully illustrated the problem with reference to a pyramid of concepts (Figure 3.1).[1] Moving down the pyramid takes increasing account of aspects of poverty that define it as a meaningful social phenomenon. In terms of measurement, the most frequently used measures lie at the top of the pyramid since they are more straightforward to operationalise.

Personal consumption is placed at the top of the pyramid, although this is typically measured with reference to personal or, more usually, household income since this is more easily measured. The concept of poverty gradually increases in scope to include shared property rights, state-provided commodities, assets, dignity and autonomy at the bottom of the pyramid. The implication of the diagram is that the various dimen-

Figure 3.1
Baulch's pyramid

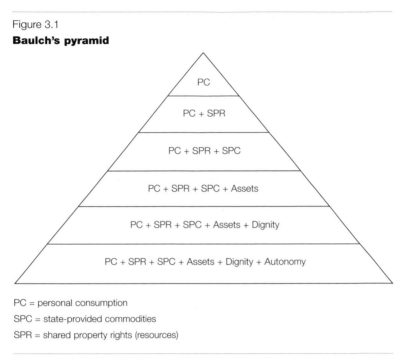

PC = personal consumption
SPC = state-provided commodities
SPR = shared property rights (resources)

Source: B Baulch, 'The New Poverty Agenda: a disputed consensus', *IDS Bulletin*, 27:1-10, 1996

sions are strictly additive, although empirically this is unlikely to be the case. Indeed, a major challenge of the current research is to formulate the nature of the relationship between these various dimensions. Moreover, it is probable that the dimensions lie in a causative sequence which will require specification.

In summary, while it is widely appreciated that poverty is an inherently multi-dimensional concept, this multi-dimensionality has generally been lost, weakened or distorted when poverty is measured. This has not just been the result of political expediency but the absence of any method by which the holistic nature of poverty can be captured in a way that facilitates measurement over time. The partial measures used to date necessarily fail to do justice to the experience of poor people and, to the extent that they distort through omission, may result in implementation of inappropriate policies.

What is required is the use of statistical techniques that represent the dimensionality of the concept in a stable fashion, an approach that will ultimately require access to comprehensive datasets with reliable measures.

A new approach to measurement

In much previous quantitative research on poverty the data reduction technique of factor analysis has been used.[2] Simply put, this technique takes a large number of indicator variables and creates a smaller number of dimensions or 'factors' by examining the correlations between the variables. These factors represent a simpler description of the data and usually can be readily interpreted by observing which variables cluster together to form the dimensions. For example, in poverty research, material deprivation scales have been created by using factor analysis on sets of items that households possess and indices developed by examining which types of item cluster together on which particular factor.

There are, however, some problems with this methodology. One is that the factor analytic techniques used in much poverty research are essentially *exploratory*. No strong theoretical justification is required in deciding which variables to include or exclude from the analysis and the researcher has little control over how the variables form the resulting factors. A second even more serious problem is that the results are sensitive to errors in the measurement of the original variables, with the result that factors are unstable over time. This means it is impossible to measure change in poverty rates because the measure of poverty is itself changing over time because of the accumulation of error.

In this research we chose to use a different, though related, technique known as structural equation modelling.[3] A structural equation model (SEM) has the potential to overcome these problems. Like factor analysis, a SEM reduces a large number of variables to a smaller number of factors. However, the technique allows measurement error to be separately identified and dealt with so that it is possible to establish trends in the incidence of multi-dimensional poverty. Unlike factor analysis, a SEM requires a strong theoretical justification before the measurement model is set up. Thus, the researcher decides which observed variables are to be associated with which factors in advance. In other words, the sorts of dimensions implied in Baulch's pyramid can be specified in advance and scores generated from data that fit those specific dimensions, assuming that appropriate data is available.[4]

Defining the measurement models

The analysis presented here utilises data from the British Household Panel Survey (BHPS). The BHPS commenced in 1991 with an initial sample of around 10,000 individuals resident in some 5,000 households. These individuals have subsequently been re-interviewed each year and the sample has also been extended to include more households from Scotland and Wales, and to embrace Northern Ireland. While the data can be weighted to provide an accurate picture of life in Great Britain or the United Kingdom at different points in time, this analysis is restricted to Great Britain (England, Scotland and Wales) to facilitate measurement of trends. The analysis covers the period 1991 to 2003 (ie, BHPS waves 1 to 13) and draws on information from adults in the study on the following topics, which are used to define the dimensions of poverty within our multi-dimensional indicators: income, finances and benefits; stress; material deprivation; general housing and neighbourhood characteristics; and social exclusion and civic participation.

While the BHPS is widely used in poverty research,[5] it has a number of shortcomings, the most important of which is that the data is not always consistent or collected for all waves. For example, the civic participation and social isolation variables are only collected in alternate waves, while the housing and neighbourhood variables were only included from 1996 onwards. Similarly, the material deprivation variables, which were limited at the beginning of the survey, were significantly augmented from 1996. Thus, we are forced to limit our analysis to alternate years (1991, 1993, 1995 etc) and to divide our analysis into two parts. The first employs a relatively simple model (referred to as Model 1) to exploit data for the full period 1991 to 2003, while the second uses a more comprehensive model that takes advantage of the better data available from 1996 onwards (referred to as Model 2). The latter model conveniently coincides with the first eight years of the Blair Government (covering years 1997, 1999, 2001 and 2003).

Finally, as with any secondary analysis, the analyst is constrained by the variables included in the dataset. Almost inevitably, key variables are omitted, while the variables available constitute only imprecise indices of the concepts of interest.

Model 1, covering the period 1991 to 2003

As noted above, the creation of a structural equation model usually relies on some strong theoretical orientation that is specified in advance. In our case, rather than a strong theory we have a pyramid-like framework of concepts that the literature suggests may be manifestations or inherent outcomes of the experience of being in poverty. Figure 3.2 presents Model 1 fitted to the BHPS data consistently available for alternative years from 1991 to 2003. The multi-dimensional poverty indicator (referred to from now on as the Poverty Index) is located in the centre of the diagram. The arrows indicate that the Poverty Index comprises the several dimensions of poverty that it is possible consistently to measure using the BHPS: financial pressure, psychological strain, social isolation and civic participation. The numbers on the diagram refer to the relative weight or importance assigned to each dimension in determining an individual's total score on the Poverty Index (the co-efficients of the model). Thus, the Poverty Index is more strongly influenced by financial strain (0.94) than by social isolation (0.33). The negative number attached to 'civic participation' is a consequence of the fact that higher civic participation is associated with low levels of poverty, causing the Poverty Index itself to be lower. In this regard, civic participation operates in the opposite direction to the other dimensions.

Some of the dimensions, notably financial pressure and psychological strain, are themselves comprised of sub-dimensions. In the former case, it can be seen (Figure 3.2) that financial pressure is more strongly influenced by financial strain, the short-term consequences of trying to make ends meet, than by material deprivation, the probable product of a sustained period of poverty. Each of the dimensions is in turn indexed by specific variables taken from the BHPS and every variable has an associated co-efficient that indicates the relative weight attached to the variable in defining the particular dimension of poverty. While the relationships between the dimensions of poverty[6] – the arrows in Figure 3.2 – were defined in advance on the basis of theory and literature, the coefficients are derived from the statistical process and reflect empirical relationships in the data. By applying 'goodness-of-fit' tests to the results of the analysis, it is possible to ensure that the SEM measurement models provide the best possible fit to the data.

Having outlined the method it is now appropriate to describe each of the major dimensions of poverty included in the model.

Figure 3.2

Model 1, 1991–2003 (waves 1–13), standardised co-efficients shown

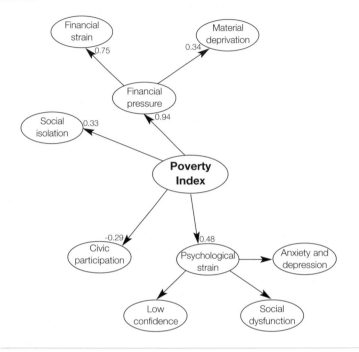

Financial strain

Several articles referred to in the previous chapter stress the importance of income-based measures of poverty, augmented here by indicators of the perceived financial situation of the household, the sense of being in financial hardship. Financial strain is an almost self-evident manifestation of poverty, certainly one that is widely documented, that comes at the top of the poverty pyramid along with income as a primary indicator of deprivation. The variables used to capture this concept include whether a housing payment had been missed in the last 12 months, whether respondents considered their financial status to be good or bad, and whether it had been getting better/worse over the last year. The intention was that these variables should capture both the medium term and the more immediate difficulties of budgeting. Income is also included on this dimension.[7]

Material deprivation

There is a large body of work on the importance of including material deprivation in any measure of poverty.[8] The measures available in the BHPS are generally limited to the ownership of certain possessions, with no reference made to whether respondents attribute lack of ownership to personal preference or inadequate resources. The raft of such indicators of material wellbeing include if the respondent's household does not possess a: CD player, VCR, washing machine, tumble dryer, microwave oven, dishwasher, personal computer, central heating, or has use of a car. Income is also included on this dimension, as well as financial strain.

We have kept material deprivation conceptually distinct from financial strain as it represents the real effects of long-term financial hardship on the household rather than the personal financial strain itself. In other words, it captures the essence of not being able to afford things or being able to replace worn-out items, such as electronic goods or kitchen appliances. Financial strain reflects monetary strain, which may be somewhat different and apply in different circumstances. For example, a household may be under financial strain because of high mortgage payments, but may have a well-equipped house. Material and financial deprivation were also linked to the Poverty Index by another latent variable representing overall financial and material deprivation. This represents the combined effects of long-term and short-term 'financial pressure'.

Social isolation

The next dimension is that of social isolation, a trait seen both as a manifestation or consequence of poverty and as a risk factor linked with downward spirals into poverty. Once a person is marginalised the effect can become self-reinforcing, as when a person no longer has friends to help them out or contacts that could help secure employment and escape poverty. The BHPS includes variables indicating whether the respondent has someone who will listen to her/him, help in a crisis, who appreciates and who comforts her/him, and with whom s/he can relax.

Civic participation

Related to social isolation, we also include the converse concept of civic participation since the literature suggests that people in poverty will often be excluded from civic participation and have weak social networks and social capital.[9] Civic participation is captured in the BHPS by two variables that count the number of organisations of which the respondent is a member and the number in which s/he is active. Respondents are presented with a list of 13 kinds of organisation from which they are asked to select ones with which they are involved. The list includes: political parties, trade unions, environmental groups, parents' associations, tenants' or residents' groups, religious groups, voluntary service organisations, community groups, social groups, sports clubs, women's institutes and women's groups. High scores indicate higher civic participation.

Psychological strain

Psychological wellbeing could be seen as a cause or a consequence of poverty.[10] There have also been a number of studies that have found an association between mental ill health and poverty.[11] We assume here that psychological strain is a component towards the bottom of our pyramid of concepts and that it can be entered into a comprehensive poverty index. Psychological strain is measured using the General Health Questionnaire set of 12 items (GHQ12)[12] split into three distinct components: low confidence, anxiety and depression, and social dysfunction.

Model 2, covering the period 1997 to 2003

The more detailed data available from 1996 onwards allows us to add another dimension, 'environment', a place-based aspect of poverty which captures housing and neighbourhood conditions, and to refine certain of the other dimensions (Figure 3.3). The housing variables included in the environment dimension are: whether the house in which a respondent resides has poor light, bad heating, leaks, rotting wood, and/or damp. Neighbourhood variables included more objective measures appertaining to noise from neighbours, noise from the street, crime levels and lack of space, and more subjective ones recording whether the respondent liked the area or not and whether s/he would prefer to move away.

The new material deprivation dimension additionally includes lack of a cable or satellite TV, together with assessments by respondents of whether they as a household could afford a week-long holiday once a year, to feed visitors once a month or to buy new clothes or replace furniture. Three extra variables were added to the social isolation dimension which recorded whether respondents reported knowing someone outside the household from whom they could borrow money or someone who might assist them find a job, or someone who might help with depression. Financial strain, civic participation and psychological strain remain as in Model 1.

Figure 3.3

Model 2, 1997–2003 (waves 7–13), standardised co-efficients shown

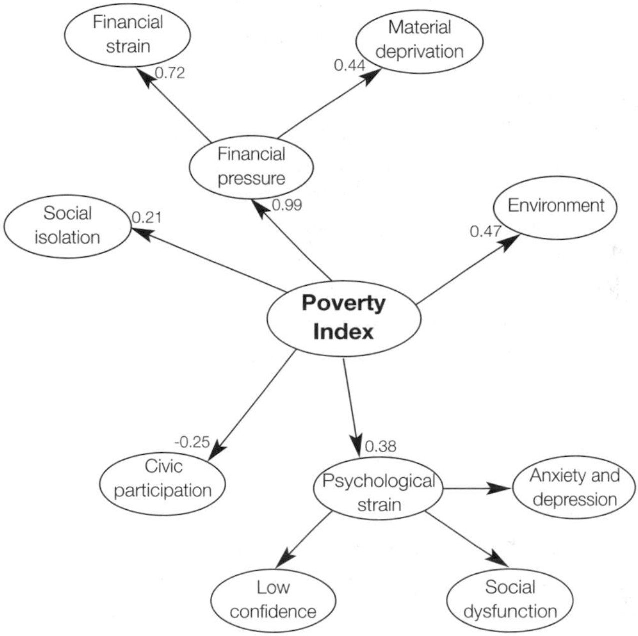

Based on the modelling, it is possible to calculate a Poverty Index score for every respondent and separate scores for each person on all the individual sub-dimensions. These were calculated from both models and form the basis of the analysis that follows.[13] Reflecting Sen's analysis of capabilities and shame discussed in Chapter 2, the overall Poverty Index reflects both absolute and relative concepts of poverty. The income measure is deflated, which removes the tendency with absolute measures for people to be floated out of poverty simply as a result of economic growth. The measures of material deprivation are socially salient but are not weighted to take account of market penetration, while indices of strain are measured in absolute terms.

Trends in multi-dimensional poverty

So what does all this modelling tell us? Does it add anything to what we might deduce by simply measuring income poverty? We believe that the answer to the second question is a profound 'yes', but first we have to explain the results and to compare them with traditional analyses.

All poverty thresholds are somewhat arbitrary. Ideally, an income-based measure would fix the threshold as the amount of income required to meet socially determined minimal needs. Conventionally, though, income-based measures are fixed as a proportion of median equivalised household income – that is, income adjusted to take account of differences in household size. The threshold for the new Poverty Index was

Figure 3.4

Percentage poor by various measures, BHPS 1991–2003

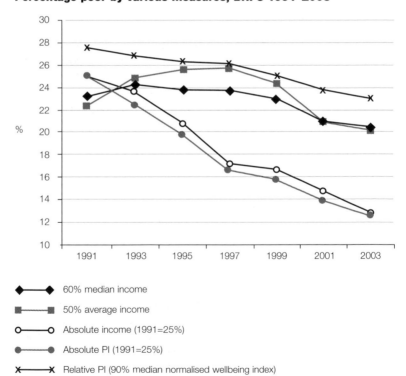

◆——◆ 60% median income

■——■ 50% average income

○══○ Absolute income (1991=25%)

●——● Absolute PI (1991=25%)

✕——✕ Relative PI (90% median normalised wellbeing index)

fixed in 1991 to ensure that 25 per cent of households fell beneath the poverty threshold, a proportion similar to the poverty rate indicated by conventional income measures (Figure 3.4). Absolute measures hold the poverty threshold constant in real terms, meaning that the threshold retains the same value in terms of the goods that could be purchased. Relative measures allow the poverty threshold to rise (or fall) with average incomes and/or overall living standards; fixing a poverty threshold as a proportion of median household income achieves this effect automatically.

Trends in the new Poverty Index are compared to conventional 'relative' and 'absolute' income poverty measures in Figure 3.4. All the measures are derived from the same BHPS data and so any differences cannot be attributed to different data. The relative income measure suggests a pattern of stable or slightly increasing poverty during the period 1992–97 when John Major was prime minister, followed by a decline after New Labour took office in 1997. In contrast, the absolute income measure, in which the poverty threshold is held constant in real terms, shows a continuous decline. This is as be expected given that the period as a whole was characterised by moderate economic growth. The absolute Poverty Index-based measure similarly shows a steady decline throughout the whole period, but so too does the relative variant.[14] Why should this be so? Because a portion of the Poverty Index is designed to capture aspects of poverty (material deprivation, for example) that are theoretically more stable and less sensitive to short-term fluctuations in the national economic situation. Not only does this more accurately reflect the actual experience of people living in poverty, it also helps to avoid the problem, noted in Chapter 2, that the observed poverty rate can sometimes appear to rise when everybody, including those counted as poor, is getting richer in times of rapid economic growth.

A Poverty Index score was calculated for every adult in the BHPS sample; the higher the score, the more severe the poverty. People with a score below 0.854 in 1991 – 75 per cent of all respondents – were not considered to be poor at all. The mean and median score from Models 1 and 2 are plotted in Figure 3.5 for all odd-numbered year waves from 1991 to 2003. This is analogous to plotting the inverse of average equivalised household income used in traditional measures since, unlike income, the Poverty Index is a direct measure of poverty and high scores indicate extreme poverty. It is evident that the mean score in Model 1 declined steadily throughout the period from around 0.43 to 0.16, which is both consistent with the recorded fall in poverty rates and also suggests a general rise in social wellbeing. The comparison between the mean and

Figure 3.5

Mean and median Poverty Index scores from the models

Model 1

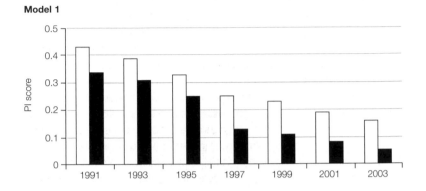

Model 2

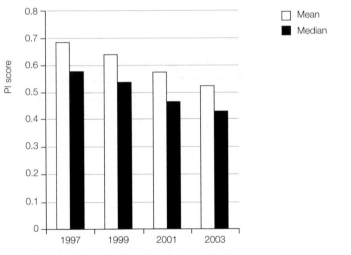

median Poverty Index is also instructive. It indicates that that the distribution of the Poverty Index is somewhat skewed, with disproportionate numbers of people having very low scores. However, the Poverty Index, which of course takes into account the many dimensions of poverty and wellbeing is less skewed and less unequal than the distribution of income alone. However, the increasing difference between the mean and median Poverty

Index scores points to a widening in social inequalities, perhaps especially during the last years of the Major Government.[15]

It is possible to estimate individuals' Poverty Index scores on all the separate dimensions of poverty and hence to calculate dimension-specific poverty rates. Again, it is necessary to select a more or less arbitrary poverty threshold for each dimension and, to ensure consistency across the dimensions, this was in each case fixed to ensure that 25 per cent of the population was defined as being poor in 1991 (Table 3.1). The material deprivation and financial strain dimensions were calculated without income included (which is presented separately), while financial pressure combines the scores for income, material deprivation and financial strain.

From Table 3.1 it can be seen that poverty rates based on the financial strain and material deprivation components of the Index both fell much faster than income, declining by three-quarters from 25 per cent in 1991 to around 8 per cent in 2003 as opposed to one-half for income. Poverty defined in terms of financial strain decreased more quickly in the early part of the period, subsequently slowing as did material deprivation, to a less marked degree, whereas the marked fall in poverty experienced as finan-

Table 3.1

Headcount poverty rates (%) using the Poverty Index and selected dimensions, Model 1, fixing the1991 rate at 25% in each case

Year	Overall	Material deprivation	Financial strain	Income	Financial pressure
1991	25	25	25	25	25
1993	23	20	16	21	22
1995	20	17	13	19	18
1997	17	14	10	16	13
1999	16	12	9	17	11
2001	14	9	8	13	9
2003	12	7	6	11	7

Headcount poverty rates (%) using the Poverty Index, Model 2, fixing the 1997 rate at 25% in each case

Year	Overall	Material deprivation	Financial strain	Income	Financial pressure	Environ- ment
1997	25	25	25	25	25	25
1999	22	21	17	23	22	23
2001	19	17	15	22	18	21
2003	17	14	14	16	15	21

cial pressure (a product of the effects of income, financial strain and material deprivation) occurred slightly later during the last years of the Major era. The other components (psychological strain, civic participation and social isolation) all remained fairly constant throughout the period and were, additionally, less closely associated in the model with the composite Poverty Index. It follows that falls in the overall Poverty Index were therefore largely due to improvements in people's material wellbeing and easing of financial strain than to changes in the social or psychological side of life.

The more comprehensive measure that it was possible to employ during the Blair era presents a subtly different picture (see Figure 3.5, Model 2). Again the mean Poverty Index score fell, but with different scaling, from 0.69 in 1997 to around 0.53 in 2003, implying an overall improvement in wellbeing. This is reflected in the headcount poverty rate, which (calculated in a fashion analogous to Model 1) fell by almost a quarter. During this period, however, while material deprivation and financial strain both fell by 44 per cent and by more than other aspects of poverty, the decline in income poverty was, though less, of a similar order of magnitude (36 per cent), presumably reflecting the significant policy shift to targeting poverty through increases in benefits and tax credits (see Table 3.1). Psychological strain, civic participation and social isolation again remained stable, but a decline in environmental or place-based poverty was evident, falling by about one-sixth from 25 to 21 per cent.

Briefly, to summarise: poverty, measured as a multi-dimensional concept, fell throughout the period 1991 to 2003 in both absolute and relative terms, driven more by reductions in material deprivation and financial strain than by increases in income *per se*. The implication is that for this period, income-based measures understated the fall in poverty. People throughout society, though particularly – as we shall see – those at the bottom, found it easier to manage and gained from increased material living standards over and above the benefits attributable to rising income. Writing in the era of the so-called international 'credit crunch', one can only wonder whether these differential experiences were to become precursors to future hardships.

The distribution of poverty

Having established trends in multi-dimensional poverty, it is important to consider its distribution and particularly which groups are most at risk.

Figure 3.6

Mean Poverty Index from Model 2 by income deciles, 1997–2003

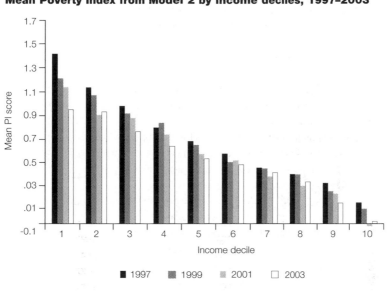

First, however, it is worth asking whether the same people are affected by multi-dimensional poverty as are afflicted by income poverty. The answer is that there is some overlap between the two groups, but that the coincidence is by no means perfect. Indeed, it will already be apparent from the structure of the SEM models and the fact that income poverty fell less markedly than other kinds of poverty, that the Poverty Index is only moderately associated with income. Typically, in any one year, the correlation between the Poverty Index and the logarithm of household equivalised income is about 0.46, with income explaining no more than around 23 per cent of the variance of the Poverty Index. This finding is, of course, consistent with Ringen's assertion (noted in Chapter 2) that income is an indirect, but also an imperfect, measure of poverty.[16] Nevertheless, the Poverty Index takes income into account and, as would be anticipated, when the BHPS sample is divided into deciles according to equivalised household income, the average Poverty Index score falls consistently with increasing income deciles (Figure 3.6).

The comparison between movements in the Poverty Index over time and changes in income is particularly instructive in that it suggests that gains in wellbeing were greatest among those with the least income, even though income inequalities were increasing throughout most of the period. Figure 3.6 not only shows that the average Poverty Index score declined for people at all points in the income distribution between 1997 and 2003, it also reveals that the biggest absolute falls occurred among the lowest income groups. Falls were especially marked for people within the lowest income decile, such that by 2003, average Poverty Index scores did not differ statistically between the first and second income deciles. However, the proportion of people in the lowest income decile that were poor according to the Poverty Index fell only marginally from 1991 to 2003, suggesting that most of the fall in the Index translated into a reduction in the severity of multi-dimensional poverty as indicated by the poverty gap – the difference between a person's Poverty Index score and the multi-dimensional poverty threshold.

Turning to the risk of experiencing multi-dimensional poverty, we find patterns, which at face value are broadly consistent with the literature on income poverty (Table 3.2). Single parents with dependent children are most at risk of poverty followed by single elderly households. Couples with children face an average risk of being poor while couples without children generally confront a low, but far from negligible, risk of poverty. These

Table 3.2

Headcount multi-dimensional poverty rates (relative %) by various household types, Model 1, 1991

	Degree of poverty		
	Severe[1]	Moderate[2]	Less severe[3]
Single, non-elderly	20	26	33
Single, elderly	18	27	39
Couple, no children	9	13	20
Couple, dependent children	13	18	26
Couple, non-dependent children	9	12	19
Lone parent, dependent children	36	48	58
Lone parent, non-dependent children	15	22	33
2+ unrelated adults	13	23	32
Other households	11	15	20
All	13	18	26

1 80% of the median Poverty Index score
2 85% of the median Poverty Index score
3 90% of the median Poverty Index score

Table 3.3

Relative risk of poverty for selected household types

	Multi-dimensional poverty			Income poverty
	Severe[1]	**Moderate**[2]	**Less severe**[3]	**60% median equivalised household income**
Single, non-elderly	154	144	127	86
Single, elderly	138	150	150	145
Couple, no children	69	72	77	52
Couple, dependent children	100	100	100	97
Lone parent, dependent children	277	267	223	197
All households	100	100	100	100

1 80% of the median Poverty Index score
2 85% of the median Poverty Index score
3 90% of the median Poverty Index score

results are what we would expect from our current understanding of the wellbeing of households. Pensioners and lone parents have the lowest standards of living in the UK and tend to live in the worst conditions. Couples with no children are the best off.

There are, though, subtle but important differences in the incidence, and hence in the risk, of experiencing multi-dimensional, as opposed to income, poverty. These are revealed when the relative risk of poverty is considered, as in Table 3.3. This shows that relative to the average, lone parents and single non-elderly people are much more prone to experience multi-dimensional poverty than income poverty. Whereas lone parents are almost twice as likely to experience income poverty as other people, they are nearly three times more likely than others to fall below the multi-dimensional poverty threshold. The turnaround is even more marked for single non-elderly people. Taking income alone, they are much less at risk of poverty than other groups, whereas taking account of all the measured dimensions of poverty they are somewhere between 25 per cent and 50 per cent more likely to be poor than the average person.

Table 3.3 also reveals that the relative risk of poverty changes slightly as the level of the multi-dimensional poverty threshold is raised from a strict or severe definition to a less severe one. The relative risk of a lone parent being poor falls as the threshold is raised, while that for single people, both elderly and non-elderly, increases. This suggests that the severity of multi-dimensional poverty is generally greater for lone parents than for the other two groups, which tends to support the Government's policy focus on lone parents.

To recap, our analysis confirms the theoretical proposition that, while income poverty is important, it fails fully to encapsulate what it means to be poor. Moreover, taking account of the non-financial dimensions of poverty reveals that the risk of poverty faced by non-elderly single people is understated when an income definition is used, while both the risk and severity of poverty experienced by lone parents is also downplayed.

Conclusions

It has long been argued that poverty is an inherently multi-dimensional concept and that reliance on one-dimensional measures can be misleading. However, it has hitherto proved impossible to devise multi-dimensional measures that are stable over time and which thereby facilitate the accurate measurement of trends in the poverty rate, a necessary requirement if the effects of anti-poverty programmes are to be assessed. Above, we have demonstrated that it is possible, through the application of structural equation modelling, to create multi-dimensional indicators without the usual drawbacks. It is also proved possible to disaggregate the contribution of the individual components to the overall trend, thereby isolating the effect of single dimensions while holding other components constant.

While we have been able to specify the dimensions of poverty, at least within the limitations of the available data, based on our understanding of the literature, it is through the empirical analysis that we have been able to specify the relative importance of each in shaping the overall experience of poverty. We discovered, as one might expect, that financial pressure lies at the heart of poverty, but importantly also that the effect of low income is mediated through short-term financial stress and longer-term material deprivation, with the former being almost twice as important as the latter. Environment emerges as the next most important dimension of poverty (although data limitations meant that this could only be measured from 1997 onwards), followed by psychological stress and, less important though still statistically significant, civic participation and social isolation. It is worth noting, as an aside, that the methodology pursued here represents a major advance on the combinatorial method recently introduced by the Government to measure child poverty and which counts people as poor if they are both income poor and experience material deprivation.[17] The Government's approach cannot adequately cope with the phenomenon that a person might often appear poor on one index and not on another, whereas we have been able to construct a single measure that takes account of a person's status on multiple dimensions of poverty, each of which can be disaggregated.

The decline in the Poverty Index between 1991 and 2003 was driven by falls in material deprivation and more especially by reduced financial stress, particularly during the early 1990s, a time when unemployment, inflation and interest rates were all falling. It is at least possible that the seeds of the current, so-called 'credit crunch' were sown at this time, with people unwittingly taking on commitments that were unsustainable, given their long-term earning power in the context of as yet unappreciated risks such as pregnancy and relationship breakdown. Further work to investigate this possibility would certainly be justified.

Interpretation of the decline in material deprivation is complex because the commodities included in the Index were fixed in 1991 (or 1997 with the inclusion of cable and satellite TV). Many of these items have become much cheaper and more widely diffused now than they would have been in 1991, with the result that one would expect the material deprivation based on these items to fall naturally during the subsequent 13 years. The implication is that, while in absolute terms the poor have become better off in that they possess more of the indicator items, they may still be experiencing relative deprivation in not having access to items that have subsequently become socially essential, such as a mobile phone. Significantly, psychological strain, social isolation and civic participation persisted at similar levels throughout the 13 years, suggesting that financial improvements in people's lives may not immediately negate the exclusionary aspects of poverty.

Finally, following others, we have demonstrated that income is only rather weakly associated with the other generally accepted manifestations of poverty.[18] Not only is this consistent with Ringen's theoretical arguments, it underlines the need to take a multi-dimensional approach seriously, not least because income measures can be misleading in the groups that appear to be most at risk of poverty.

Notes

1 B Baulch, 'The New Poverty Agenda: a disputed consensus', *IDS Bulletin* 27, 1996, pp1-10

2 See for example, M Calandrino, *Low Income and Deprivation in British Families*, DWP Working Paper 10, Department for Work and Pensions, 2003 and T

Haase and J Pratschke, *Deprivation and its Spatial Articulation in the Republic of Ireland*, ADM Ltd /NDP, 2005

3   Although SEM has rarely been used in the measurement of poverty, we are aware of the following exceptions: R Layte, B Nolan and C Whelan, 'Targeting Poverty: lessons from monitoring Ireland's national anti-poverty strategy', *Journal of Social Policy* 29(4), 2000, pp553-75; W Kuklys, 'Measuring Standards of Living in the UK: an application of Sen's functioning approach using structural equation models', *Working Paper on Strategic Interaction* 11, Max Planck Institute, Jena, 2004; T Haase and J Pratschke, *Deprivation and its Spatial Articulation in the Republic of Ireland*, ADM Ltd/NDP, 2005; and MSD, *Direct Measurement of Living Standards: the New Zealand ELSI Scale*, New Zealand Ministry of Social Development, 2002

4   A much more detailed and technical exposition of the models presented in this chapter can be found in M Tomlinson, R Walker and G Williams, 'Measuring Poverty in Britain as a Multi-dimensional Concept 1991 to 2003', *Journal of Social Policy* 37(4), 2008

5   For example, SP Jenkins and J Rigg, *The Dynamics of Poverty in Britain*, DWP Research Report 157, Corporate Document Services, 2001; J Ermisch, M Francesconi and DJ Pevalin, *Outcomes for Children of Poverty*, DWP Research Report 158, Corporate Document Services, 2001; SP Jenkins and L Cappellari, 'Summarising Multiple Deprivation Indicators', in SP Jenkins and J Micklewright (eds), *Inequality and Poverty Re-examined*, Oxford University Press, 2007, pp166-84

6   More detail can be found in M Tomlinson, R Walker and G Williams, 'Measuring Poverty in Britain as a Multi-dimensional Concept 1991 to 2003', *Journal of Social Policy* 37(4), 2008. The details of the statistical models are available from the Oxford Research Archive at: http://ora.ouls.ox.ac.uk. For simplicity, neither the variables nor the associated co-efficients are shown in Figure 3.2.

7   After considerable experimentation, gross income was used instead of the theoretically more appropriate measure of disposable income. The decision led to 10 per cent fewer cases being dropped from some of the analyses on account of missing values. All the indices and sub-indices are very highly correlated when the different income measures are used and poverty rates differ by less than a percentage point across the various demographic subgroups.

8   SP Jenkins and L Cappellari, 'Summarising Multiple Deprivation Indicators', in SP Jenkins and J Micklewright (eds), *Inequality and Poverty Re-examined*, Oxford University Press, 2007, pp166-84; C Whelan and B Maitre, 'Vulnerability and Multiple Deprivation Perspectives on Economic Exclusion in Europe: a latent class analysis', *European Societies* 7(3), 2005, pp423-50; M Willetts, *Measuring Child Poverty Using Material Deprivation: possible approaches*, DWP Working Paper 28, Corporate Document Services, 2006

9   V Cattell, 'Poor People, Poor Places and Poor Health: the mediating role of social networks and social capital', *Social Science and Medicine* 52, 2001, pp1501-16; D Gordon and others, *Poverty and Social Exclusion in Britain*, Joseph Rowntree Foundation, 2000; C Pantazis, D Gordon and R Levitas (eds), *Poverty and Social Exclusion in Britain: the Millennium survey*, The Policy Press, 2006

10 For example, S Payne, 'Mental Health, Poverty and Social Exclusion', in C Pantazis, D Gordon and R Levitas (eds), *Poverty and Social Exclusion in Britain: the Millennium survey*, The Policy Press, 2006

11 For instance, S Weich and G Lewis, 'Poverty, Unemployment and Common Mental Disorders: population-based cohort study', *British Medical Journal* 317, 1998, pp115-19; and E Whitley, D Gunnell, D Dorling and GD Smith, 'Ecological Study of Social Fragmentation, Poverty and Suicide', *British Medical Journal* 319, 1999, pp1034-37

12 Following M Shevlin and G Adamson, 'Alternative Factor Models and Factorial Invariance of the GHQ-12: a large sample analysis using confirmatory factor analysis', *Psychological Assessment* 17(2), 2005, pp231-36, we modelled psychological strain as a three-part model combining anxiety/depression (items 2, 5, 6, 9), social dysfunction (1, 3, 4, 7, 8) and loss of confidence (10 and 11). This produces a much better fit than using all 12 items loading on just one latent variable.

13 More detail can be found in M Tomlinson, R Walker and G Williams, 'Measuring Poverty in Britain as a Multi-dimensional Concept 1991 to 2003', *Journal of Social Policy* 37(4), 2008. The details of the statistical models are available from the Oxford Research Archive at: http://ora.ouls.ox.ac.uk. For simplicity, neither the variables nor the associated co-efficients are shown in Figure 3.2.

14 See Appendix for the calculation of the relative version of Poverty Index.

15 It is not possible to assess straightforwardly the strength of the fall in the Poverty Index because the scores are not standardised in any way. Moreover, since a negative score is possible, meaning that a score of zero does not indicate an absence of poverty, it cannot be presumed that that the average Poverty Index more than halved.

16 S Ringen, 'Direct and Indirect Measures of Poverty', *Journal of Social Policy* 17(3), 1988, pp351-65

17 Department for Work and Pensions, *Measuring Child Poverty*, Department for Work and Pensions, 2003

18 R Berthoud, M Blekesaune and R Hancock, *Are 'Poor' Pensioners 'Deprived'?*, DWP Research Report 364, Corporate Document Services, 2006; R Berthoud, M Bryan and E Bardasi, *The Dynamics of Deprivation: the relationship between income and material deprivation over time*, DWP Research Report 219, Corporate Document Services, 2004

Four

The dynamics of multi-dimensional poverty

Introduction

We saw, in the previous chapter, that poverty fell throughout the period 1991 and 2003, which means that significant numbers of people moved out of poverty. Indeed, in reality many more people will have escaped from poverty than is suggested by the fall in the poverty rate from 27.5 per cent to 23 per cent. This is because, while some people left poverty, others will have become poor for the first time and yet others will have moved in and out of poverty on several occasions. It is now widely recognised that it is just as important to study these poverty dynamics as it is to measure poverty rates. However, most studies of poverty dynamics have concerned income poverty and little is known about the dynamics of poverty when it is defined in multi-dimensional terms.

Moreover, previous studies of dynamics have tended to focus on estimating the duration and number of spells of poverty experienced by people over comparatively short periods of time. This chapter takes a much longer-term view of poverty and uses methods that seek to explain the determinants of poverty trajectories followed by individuals over 14 years (and measured in a multi-dimensional fashion).[1] This analysis allows for a deeper understanding of the processes that shape people's experience of poverty over substantial portions of their lives, which in turn can be used to inform thinking about policy options.

It is the increasing availability of longitudinal data, most notably the UK cohort studies and the British Household Panel Survey (BHPS), which has made possible the study of poverty dynamics.[2] The studies have demonstrated that poverty is much more widespread than indicated by cross-sectional statistics, but also that it is more complex. Few people are permanently poor, but many experience repeated spells of poverty. Transient, recurrent and permanent poverty may differ in kind, in their effects on the individuals involved and in their consequences for society as a whole. The risk events associated with poverty are more prevalent than actual spells of poverty, which suggests that social structures, and individual agency and government policies may protect some people against the onset of poverty.

In Chapter 3 we used the BHPS to track long-term trends in the multi-dimensional Poverty Index. In this chapter, we use the same data to explore individual histories over the same time period (1991 to 2003) and to investigate the inherent causes or determinants of poverty from a multi-dimensional perspective. By adopting a long-term perspective we identify the factors that trigger sustained downward trajectories into poverty (or long-term moves out of poverty) rather than the episodic events which, though important in the short term, may have consequences that evaporate quite quickly. We also explore which social groups risk experiencing long-term poverty, with a view to thinking about the targeting of preventive interventions.

Policy targeting in the UK

As already discussed, the current Labour administration has focused particular attention on child poverty in Britain and pledged to eradicate it by 2020. Policy continues to evolve rapidly, but the steps the Government believes to be necessary to reduce child poverty, as set out in *The Child Poverty Review* in 2004, remain relevant:[3]

- Increase employment opportunities, raising incomes for those who can work.
- Increase support for those who cannot work.
- Improve the effectiveness of public services that tackle material deprivation, for instance, housing and homelessness.
- Improve those public services – for example, education, that can contribute most to increasing the future life chances of children in households with low incomes, and ensure public services and the welfare system work well together when families face crisis points in their lives.
- Improve services for children and their families living in deprived areas, including targeted programmes.

This policy agenda is embedded in, and reflects, a broader policy thrust with three key characteristics. The first is the strong emphasis on employment as the principal way out of poverty, leading to the sustained investment in successive generations of welfare-to-work (or activation) policies, designed to encourage an ever greater number of benefit recipients to enter or return to work.[4] A second characteristic, evident in the welfare-to-work programmes, but also apparent more widely in government rhetoric, is the juxtaposition of rights and responsibilities. Sometimes these notions are conflated as they are in the context of poverty and employment; while it is presumed to be the right of anyone to expect a minimum standard of living, it is also presumed to be an individual's responsibility to seek gainful employment in order to meet that end. A third feature, corresponding with the first two bullet points above, is a strong emphasis on helping families (single parents in particular) financially by means of the tax credit and benefit systems.[5]

While the Conservative opposition shares the Government's ambitions on child poverty, its policy perspectives (insofar as they can be ascertained) are rather different. However, they have made clear their belief in the need for a stable family environment (by which is generally meant a two-parent family) in order to fight child poverty. Their proposals emphasise help for couples with children and encouraging couples to stay together as a family unit as a means of alleviating the risks to children.[6]

This policy context helps shape our analysis of poverty dynamics since the longitudinal panel data at our disposal allows us to explore the impact of employment, labour force status and family circumstances – and changes in these factors – on our multi-dimensional indicator over the long term. This approach strikes us as being particularly apposite, given the difficulty of reaching the child poverty targets under current fiscal conditions.[7]

Because of data limitations, it is more difficult to assess the impact of government services, education and housing in the same way. For example, we know that many poor families are homeless or live in temporary accommodation, but these people will not be picked up adequately in our data. Furthermore, the long-term impacts of education reforms on a child's future chances are also difficult to measure and beyond the scope of the present work.

Modelling poverty experiences over the long term

The approach that we adopt in the analysis is called 'latent growth modelling'. In essence, a latent growth model takes a repeated measure of an indicator, such as our Poverty Index, and creates two measures that summarise the level and the trajectory of the indicator for every individual in the sample. Each individual in the analysis can be thought of as having a baseline score measured by the indicator (referred to as the *intercept*) and a trajectory representing how the individual's score generally changes over time (usually referred to as the *slope*).

In our case, the Poverty Index was measured at two-year intervals between 1991 and 2003 and a latent growth model applied measuring the change in our Index over this period. The estimation of the intercepts gives us a measure of the long-term, baseline severity of poverty for each person in the sample, while the slopes provide measures of the long-term poverty trajectory of every individual. Figure 4.1 shows some hypothetical cases of individuals with different intercepts and slopes related to the Poverty Index measured between 1991 and 2003 in the BHPS. An individual with a high intercept value generally experiences deep or severe poverty over much of the time period. Individuals with a high positive or negative slope value tend, respectively, to become worse or better off.

Taking this modelling a stage further, we can explore the significant determinants of individuals' poverty baselines and trajectories while simultaneously taking many things into account. We can also investigate whether particular circumstances or events trigger a move in or out of poverty or a change in the severity of poverty. In the long run, it is possible that this approach could assist in the fight against poverty by enabling the relative significance of various triggers of poverty to be assessed and by helping target support and assistance to people at risk of long-term poverty.

We estimated two models for people of working age. The first explored the characteristics of individuals and households that might be thought to make them more or less prone to poverty. Some characteristics that do not change, gender for example, were measured only once at the beginning of the study period but others were measured afresh in each of the years studied. The second model added selected household events to help isolate the significant triggers that might push a family or individual over the edge into poverty.[8]

No statistical model is perfect and the variables available are frequently depressingly imprecise, adding to the difficulty of choosing which variables to include in the analysis and which to exclude. Our analysis was no different. Among the individual and household characteristics that we included were gender and ethnicity, occupation, employment status and family situation (Table 4.1). Full-time occupation was disaggregated into

Figure 4.1

Hypothetical examples of poverty trajectories using the latent growth model

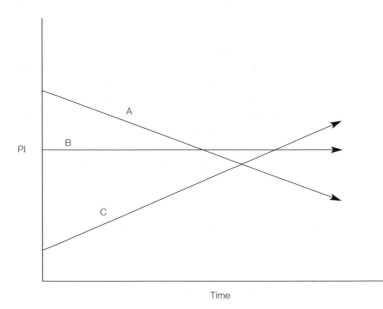

A represents a person who starts off poor but gradually gets better off
B represents someone whose poverty stays the same throughout the observation period
C represents someone who descends into poverty

six status categories, ranging from semi and unskilled work to profession-al, while part-time employment was separated into just two types (higher and lower status[9]). People not working were divided into those who were unemployed, carers (a person who is not working, but not looking for work because of other family circumstances), and those who were long-term sick or disabled. A variable was also included to indicate whether the person had a partner who was employed. Family circumstances were represented as one of six states corresponding to various stages in the life history of a family: single people, couples with no children, couples with dependent children, couples with non-dependent children, lone parents with dependants and lone parents with non-dependants. In order to explore the impact of changes in household composition that might act as triggers to induce spells of poverty, we included simple changes in the family situation alongside the occupation and employment variables rather than family status *per se*. Specifically, we examined the impact of increases in the number of dependent children, the separation of couples and family formation – ie, the transition from being a single adult household to sharing a household with a partner.

The results of the analysis are presented in Tables 4.1 and 4.2. The presence of a '+' or '–' sign in the tables indicates a statistically significant change in the Index across all or most of the period under observation (1991 to 2003). Thus, a '+' indicates a significant increase in people's Poverty Index score (and therefore an increase in the severity of their poverty) and a '–' indicates a reduction in the Index and hence in the severity of poverty. While we examined both the severity of poverty experienced by people and their trajectories, our results are largely concerned with the former. This is because, for the most part, the variables considered did not significantly affect trajectories in the same way as they helped to explain differences in the severity of poverty. However, it should be remembered that the models used separate the effects the variables have on the severity of poverty from the effects they have on movements in and out of poverty.

Understanding long-term poverty

The analysis confirms that full-time employment serves as a very strong defence against poverty, which is, of course, consistent with the Government's emphasis on welfare-to-work programmes. Moreover, as one might have expected (although it is not shown in the tables), the degree of protection increases with the status of the employment: people in professional and managerial employment have much lower Poverty Index scores than skilled manual workers who, in turn, have lower scores than semi and unskilled workers. Having two people in a family working also has a very strong protective effect with very few such families falling below the poverty line in any of years covered by the study.

However, part-time employment in itself generally offers very little protection against poverty over the long term. Only when the higher-status part-time occupations are broken down into more detailed categories does it become apparent that managerial and professional positions have a downward influence on the Poverty Index. Having a routine and unskilled part-time job had no significant effect at all on the Poverty Index in many of the models that were explored. Being unemployed

Table 4.1

A model with gender, ethnicity, occupation, employment status and household type

Female	+
Non-white	+
Employment:	
Full-time professional/manager	−
Full-time routine white collar	−
Full-time self-employed	−
Full-time personal service	−
Full-time foreman/technician	−
Full-time skilled manual	−
Full-time semi and unskilled	−
Part-time higher-status job	−
Part-time lower-status job	−
Unemployed	+
Carer	+
Long-term sick/disabled	+
Partner employed	−
(Base: relative to other unoccupied categories)	
Household type:	
Single adult	+
Couple	ns
Couple + dependent children	ns
Couple + non-dependent children	ns
Lone parent + dependent children	+
Lone parent + non-dependent children	+ from 1999 onwards
(Base: relative to other household types)	

+ indicates a significant positive effect
− indicates a significant negative effect
ns indicates not statistically significant

though, or being a carer or having long-term illness or disability, all significantly increase the risk of poverty over the long term, with unemployed and disabled people being noticeably more disadvantaged than carers.

While some forms of employment protect against poverty, over the longer term certain types of household appear to be very exposed to multi-dimensional poverty, notably single people and lone parents

Table 4.2

A model with gender, race, occupation, employment status and household events triggering change

Female	+
Non-white	+
Employment:	
Full-time service class	–
Full-time routine white collar	–
Full-time self-employed	–
Full-time personal service	–
Full-time foreman/technician	–
Full-time skilled manual	–
Full-time semi and unskilled	–
Part-time higher status	–
Part-time lower status	ns
Unemployed	+
Carer	+
Long-term sick/disabled	+
Partner employed	–
(Base: relative to other unoccupied categories)	
Household event:	
Increased number of children	+ from 1997 onwards
Couple separation	+
Couple formation	ns

+ indicates a significant positive effect
– indicates a significant negative effect
ns indicates not statistically significant

(whether with dependent children or not). Moreover, relationship breakdown and associated separation very significantly increase the chances of suffering from severe poverty in the longer term for both partners, with the increased risk being considerably greater for women than for men (Table 4.2). Perhaps a little surprisingly, forming a partnership does not seem to alter the long-term risk of poverty, while having more children only seems to have had an effect – to increase the likelihood of poverty – since 1997, which may be a reflection of changes to child benefit and the introduction of tax credits, which increased payments to first children relative to others.

Finally, gender and ethnicity appear to have a significant impact on the risk of experiencing poverty over the long term, even after account is taken of differences in household type, occupation and household changes. Not being white in Britain during the 1990s and early 2000s carried a major penalty in terms of the increased risk of poverty, one that was, in fact, three times greater than that associated with being a woman. Both being non-white and being a woman increased the risk of severe poverty, but neither affected the likely trajectory out of poverty once other factors had been taken into consideration.

To summarise, the groups who seem to confront the highest long-term risk of poverty are:

- single people;
- lone parents;
- people who are not working (especially when unemployed, or sick or disabled);
- people working in low-status occupations (typically attracting lower wages and offering less advantageous terms of employment), especially if part time;
- people from households in which a couple has recently separated;
- women;
- people from minority ethnic communities.

Family or employment?

To return to the policy focus on employment and on the family, the first thing to note is that, although employment generally serves to lower the risk of experiencing poverty, lone-parent families and single childless people are still much more prone to poverty than other types of family, even when differences in employment are taken into account. In order to assess the extent to which employment can lower the risk of poverty for these two relatively disadvantaged groups, it is necessary to return to the statistical models and to compare the size of the relevant co-efficients (Tables 4.3 and 4.4). To make comparison easier, the numbers are standardised to show the relative effect of the various individual and household characteristics on the multi-dimensional Poverty Index. To simplify matters still further, the figures are shown are for the latest year only (2003), although these are generally representative of all the years studied.[10]

From Table 4.3 it can seen that the two largest positive coefficients,

Table 4.3

Selected impact size relating to 2003

Full-time service class	−0.240
Full-time routine white collar	−0.130
Full-time personal service	−0.047 (ns)
Full-time self-employed	−0.143
Full-time foreman/technician	−0.146
Full-time skilled manual	−0.130
Full-time semi/unskilled	−0.116
Part-time high status	−0.140
Part-time low status	−0.005 (ns)
Single	0.106 (ns)
Couple, no children	0.000 (ns)
Couple, dependants	0.079 (ns)
Couple, non-dependants	−0.002 (ns)
Lone parent, dependants	0.229
Lone parent, non-dependants	0.257

ns = not statistically significant

signifying an increase in the risk and severity of poverty, are both associated with being a lone parent, either with or without dependent children.
Moreover, there is only one negative coefficient of similar size, namely that
associated with 'service class' employment, which covers managerial and
professional occupations. What this means is that the risk of severe poverty associated with being a lone parent can only be offset if the lone parent secures full-time employment in the most prestigious and lucrative
kind of occupation. Self-employment and full-time employment in semi
and unskilled occupations lower the Poverty Index, as does part-time
employment in higher-status occupations, but not by nearly enough to
alleviate the pressures of being a single parent. Personal service occupations and part-time lower status occupations make hardly any difference
at all.

Therefore, employment offers no guaranteed pathway out of poverty for lone parents; only full-time employment in the best of jobs can
achieve this. Moreover, the fact that lone parents remain substantially disadvantaged, even when their live-in children are supposedly financially
independent, points to the need to take more account of the long-term
consequences of lone parenthood. The impact of relationship breakdown

Table 4.4

Selected impact size relating to 2003

Full-time service class	−0.242
Full-time routine white collar	−0.137
Full-time personal service	−0.043 (ns)
Full-time self-employed	−0.145
Full-time foreman/technician	−0.166
Full-time skilled manual	−0.128
Full-time semi/unskilled	−0.112
Part-time high status	−0.141
Part-time low status	−0.012 (ns)
Increased number of children	0.096
Couple separation	0.347
Couple formation	0.004 (ns)

ns = not statistically significant

and separation on the risk of poverty is evident from Table 4.4. Separation significantly increases the size of the Poverty Index, irrespective of occupational status and it would seem that even the most prestigious employment cannot fully offset the increased risk of poverty over the longer term. On the other hand, employment does appear to offer single childless adults substantial protection against poverty, but for most part this would entail a person securing a full-time job.

Conclusions

Whereas in the previous chapter we documented national trends in the multi-dimensional poverty rate between 1991 and 2003, in this chapter we have focused on individual trajectories over the same period and sought to identify events and characteristics that might make individuals more prone to poverty over the long term. In so doing, our approach has been influenced both by the belief among policy makers that employment offers the best route out of poverty and by the increased attention being paid by the official opposition to the family as a defence against poverty. Our conclusions are that, while employment is important, it is not a universal panacea, and that, although family breakdown is a major cause of poverty, there is little evidence that family formation or reconstitution does much to lift individuals out of poverty over the longer term.

The consequences of relationship breakdown and separation in increasing the susceptibility to multi-dimensional poverty are very marked, affecting, as they do, both men and, particularly, women. Moreover, given that our observations were necessarily spaced at two-year intervals, we will have missed many of the short-term effects of separation on poverty, while demonstrating that the impact is sustained over considerable periods. Indeed, the finding that lone parents are still massively at risk of poverty even after their children have notionally attained financial independence underlines the long-term consequences of relationship breakdown. Furthermore, as we show in the next chapter, a stable home environment is one of the key determinants of child wellbeing along a number of dimensions.

Unlike studies in the United States, we did not uncover evidence of symmetry in the dissolution and formation of relationships.[11] It does not seem that in Britain it is generally possible to 'marry' one's way out of poverty by partnering, at least not as evidenced by the period between 1991 and 2003. New unions that were formed appeared to have no significant effect on the risk of poverty for either of the individuals involved. Therefore, while in policy terms it might be possible to prevent occurrences of poverty by reducing relationship breakdown (although how this would be done, and with what other consequences, is unclear), there is no basis for believing that encouraging partnering or marriage would have much impact on the long-term poverty rate. On the other hand, it is clear that, despite all the policy innovation witnessed during the 1990s and early 2000s, lone parents remain very susceptible to poverty over long periods and, hence, that new policy thinking is required.

Policy thinking to date has focused largely, if not exclusively, on employment as a bulwark against poverty. Self-evidently, paid work can make a real difference, although its effect on the various dimensions of poverty is likely to vary both in timing and in degree. Moreover, employment alone seems insufficient to lift most lone parents out of long-term poverty. This is because only full-time employment in a high status job is likely to generate the resources necessary to compensate for the losses due to relationship breakdown and the costs of lone parenthood. The low-skilled, low-paid employment generally available to lone parents proves likely to be of real benefit only if it proves to be stable and to be a stepping stone to better long-term prospects – the exception rather than the rule, given that low-skilled and personal service jobs tend to be low paid, temporary and inherently unstable. It is not surprising, therefore, that a significant number of participants in the New Deal for Lone Parents have moved into poor quality employment, with high exit rates and quite rapidly returned to benefits.[12]

Finally, two other results are worth underlining. First, to be single and alone is not necessarily to be poor, but the risk of people with these characteristics experiencing multi-dimensional poverty over the longer term is noticeably higher than for most other groups. The vulnerability of this group has been noted in the context of cross-sectional measures of poverty and at various times they have been a policy priority. Alongside tackling child poverty, policy makers should be concerned about the living conditions and health of working-age adults living alone without children.

Secondly, our analysis hints at the probable continued existence of discrimination in relation to gender and ethnicity. Certainly, like income poverty in the here and now, multi-dimensional poverty observed over long periods is contoured by ethnicity and gender.

Notes

1   The methodology (latent growth modelling) is a powerful tool that can be used to understand simultaneously both short- and long-term determinants of poverty trajectories.

2   See for example, R Walker with K Ashworth, *Poverty Dynamics: issues and examples*, Avebury, 1994; S Jenkins and J Rigg, *The Dynamics of Poverty in Britain*, DWP Working Paper 157, Corporate Document Services, 2001; J Rigg and T Sefton, 'Income Dynamics and the Life Cycle', *Journal of Social Policy* 35(3), 2006, pp411-35; G Maggio, *Multidimensional Analysis Of Poverty Dynamics In Great Britain*, Working Papers of the Institute for Social and Economic Research, Paper 10, University of Essex, 2004; D Fouarge and R Layte, 'Welfare Regimes and Poverty Dynamics: the duration and recurrence of poverty spells in Europe', *Journal of Social Policy* 34(3), 2005, pp407-26; R Layte and C Whelan, 'Moving in and out of Poverty: the impact of welfare regimes on poverty dynamics in the EU', *European Societies* 5(2), 2003, pp167-91; C Whelan, R Layte and B Maitre, 'Multiple Deprivation and Persistent Poverty in the European Union', *Journal of European Social Policy* 12(2), 2002, pp91-105

3   HM Treasury, *The Child Poverty Review*, HMT/HMSO, 2004, p5

4   See D Hirsch, *What Will it Take to End Child Poverty? Firing on all cylinders*, Joseph Rowntree Foundation, 2006, Chapter 2 for an overview and a discussion of the limitations of this approach.

5 Department for Work and Pensions, *Working for Children*, Cm 7067, The Stationery Office, 2007

6 For example, S Callan and others, *The State of the Nation Report: fractured families*, Social Policy Justice Group, 2006

7 See for example, M Brewer, J Brown and H Sutherland, *Micro-simulating Child Poverty in 2010 and 2020*, Joseph Rowntree Foundation, 2006

8 The models were estimated for the whole sample of individuals where complete data was available for all waves. Furthermore, the event model excluded Wave 1 (as these models are based on events happening between waves, we cannot include Wave 1 as we do not have enough information on what happened to the household before 1991).

9 Higher status includes professionals, managers, self-employed, foremen and technicians, skilled manual; lower status is routine white collar, personal service, semi and unskilled.

10 These relate only to the last wave of data in the analysis (Wave 13 from 2003), but are fairly representative of the results from all the other waves.

11 M Rank, *One Nation, Underprivileged: why American poverty affects us all*, Oxford University Press, 2004. But see also T Mauldin and Y Mimura, 'Marrying, Unmarrying and Poverty Dynamics among Mothers with Children Living at Home', *Journal of Family and Economic Issues* 28(4), 2007, pp566-82

12 A Yeo, 'Experience of Work and Job Retention Among Lone Parents: an evidence review', DWP Working Paper 37, Corporate Document Services, 2007

Five

Children's experience of poverty

In Chapter 3 we not only showed that it was technically possible to capture the complexity of poverty as adults experience it but also that the incidence of poverty measured in this way declined noticeably between 1991 and 2003 in both absolute and relative terms. The fall was initially driven by a drop in the level of financial stress, people's ability to cope financially and, subsequently, by falls in material deprivation as goods became relatively cheaper. Incomes rose, but respondents' rounded experiences of life improved even more, thereby lifting greater numbers of people above the poverty line when measured in a multi-dimensional way than when measured by income alone.

The focus of attention shifts in this chapter away from adults to children. We do not seek directly to measure the dimensions of childhood poverty (although in Chapter 6 we investigate the wellbeing of children based on questionnaires completed by young people aged 11 to 15). Rather, we pay attention to children living in households headed by a person with a multi-dimensional poverty score below the poverty threshold. It is, of course, possible that some heads of household are both able and choose to make sacrifices of varying kinds to ensure that their children do not experience the full force of the household's poverty.[1] It may also be the case that some children in apparently more prosperous households will experience poverty either inadvertently through poor budgeting or as a result of wanton neglect. However, logic suggests that the probability of a child experiencing poverty is much increased if adults in the households are themselves poor.

The extent of child poverty

It is widely recognised that children are more at risk of poverty than adults. This reflects the fact that all children, other than the small number cared for in institutions, live in families in which income has to be shared between adults and children. Many adults – indeed the majority of adults – live in households without children and so do not have to spend any of their income meeting the needs of children. Since the main forms of income (wages, investment income and certain benefits) are not determined by household size or need, adults without children are typically better off than adults with children and hence, parental sacrifice notwithstanding, better off than children themselves. In addition, adults who manage to follow the traditional career trajectory of rising incomes are likely to find themselves with most income at the time when their children have left home and ostensibly have become independent of parental resources.

The threshold for the multi-dimensional measure of poverty was arbitrarily fixed at 25 per cent of adults in 1991 and this poverty rate fell over time to 12 per cent in 2003 (Figure 5.1). The corresponding figures for children were respectively 30 per cent and 13 per cent, indicating not only that the incidence of child poverty fell as did that for adults, but that the increased risk of poverty faced by children over adults was noticeably reduced, from 20 per cent in 1991 to just 11 per cent 2003. The good news, then, is that multi-dimensional poverty among children fell at an even faster rate than among adults.

Figure 5.1

Poverty rates for children and adults

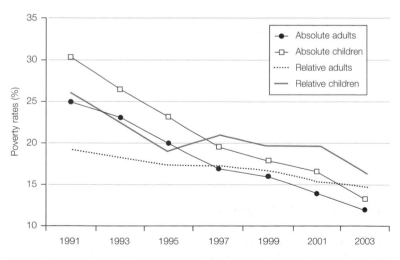

When measured in relative terms, of course, the adult poverty rate proved to be more stubborn, partly because of the well-documented increase in inequality that occurred over the 1990s and into the first years of the twenty-first century. Among adults, multi-dimensional poverty measured in a relative sense[2] fell from 19 per cent to 15 per cent between 1991 and 2003, whereas that for children fell markedly faster, from 26 per cent to 16 per cent. While the absolute poverty rates for adults and children tracked each other downwards over the period, the relative rate for children appeared to exaggerate movements in the adult rate. Relative poverty for children fell very rapidly between 1991 and 1995 but, while the adult rate remained more or less constant from then until 2001, that for children rose until 1997, then hesitated, before falling sharply between 2001 and 2003. This sharp decline, when absolute and relative poverty among children fell at a similar rate, coincided with the maturation of a number of anti-child poverty measures triggered by the Government's 1999 commitment to eradicating child poverty. Possibly reflecting the Government's change in emphasis, adult poverty – again measured relatively – scarcely changed between 2001 and 2003, whereas the rate for children fell by 3.4 percentage points, or 17 per cent.

The fall in relative child poverty identified by the multi-dimensional measure was noticeably more than that registered by simple income-based measures. So, while over the period 1991 to 2003, relative income poverty fell by almost one-quarter from 28.6 to 21.6 per cent, multi-dimensional poverty also measured relatively declined by nearly two-fifths – from 26 per cent to 16.4 per cent. By looking at movements in the other dimensions of poverty it is possible to understand why this should be so (Figure 5.2).

In 1991, as already noted, children faced a noticeably greater risk than adults of living in households characterised by multi-dimensional poverty. Figure 5.2 shows that they were also more likely to live in households with equivalent incomes below 60 per cent of the median and in which the head of household reported financial stress, indexed by indebtedness and self-assessment of their financial circumstances. In the subsequent 12 years, income poverty fell noticeably after an initial rise, while financial stress declined earlier and progressed further, contributing substantially to the fall in the overall index of multi-dimensional poverty. Families found it easier to cope financially in the early twenty-first century than they had a decade or so earlier.

What was particularly noticeable in 1991, and remained true throughout the period studied, was that children were very unlikely to live

Figure 5.2

Trends in the dimensions of child poverty

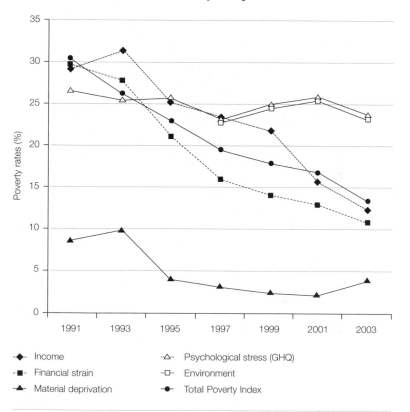

-◆- Income

-■- Financial strain

-▲- Material deprivation

-△- Psychological stress (GHQ)

-□- Environment

-●- Total Poverty Index

in households experiencing material deprivation. In part, this may point to problems with the way in which material deprivation is measured – ie, by the absence of consumer durables such as a washing machine, tumble drier, central heating, CD player and personal computer. The data source, the British Household Panel Survey (BHPS), does not include questions asking respondents about whether they would like to own the consumer durables they do not have, if they could afford them. It may be, therefore, that the index of material deprivation partly measures consumption preferences rather than hardship.

On the other hand, the finding underlines the importance that parents attach to consumer goods, such as washing machines and tumble driers, that make servicing children's basic needs more manageable, and to letting children have access to electronic equipment that can provide entertainment, education or both.[3] As many as 76 per cent of single elderly people fell beneath the deprivation threshold, which suggests both life-cycle and a cohort dimension to material deprivation since many of the products included in the index have been introduced as consumer products comparatively recently. Just 7.6 per cent of households with children and 8.7 per cent of children as a whole were defined as being materially deprived compared with 20 per cent of childless couples of working age. This latter finding points not only to the additional costs that have come to be associated with bringing up children, but also in social, if not absolute, terms, to the extreme relative deprivation likely to be experienced by the small number of children living in households without access to such social necessities as central heating, a washing machine and a personal computer.

Interestingly, children are marginally less likely to live in a household in which the head reports symptoms of psychological stress. Whether this is attributable to the beneficial mental health effects of being a parent or due to selectivity, with less stressed people having, or being able to have, children, is not discernable from the data. Analysis of the 1999 Poverty and Social Exclusion survey, smaller in scale than the BHPS and less statistically robust, found that couple parents were no more or less likely than other adults to exhibit symptoms of psychological stress but lone parents were more prone to report symptoms of depression than any other demographic group.[4] This study also found that lone parents were more likely than other adults to suffer from psychological stress but this was offset by the mental wellbeing of couple parents and the fact that more children lived with two adults than with a lone parent.

While the 1999 Poverty and Social Exclusion survey focuses on adults, Figure 5.2 concerns children and there is reason to believe that parents with more than one child – in which children by definition are over-represented – exhibit less stress, being older, more experienced and less likely to be a lone parent. What the 1999 Poverty and Social Exclusion survey also cannot reveal is the change in the level of parental stress over time. Figure 5.2 shows that, despite the strong contribution of psychological stress to the overall measure of multi-dimensional poverty, the probability of a child living with stressed parents did not decline systematically between 1991 and 2003 despite the marked fall in poverty. One conceivable explanation is that psychological stress that is part of poverty is more a product of relative, rather than absolute, differences in deprivation. So, for example, parents in poverty may be less stressed as a result of an absolute shortage of money than by not being able to buy the latest toys for their children, or to participate fully in social activities or live up to current expectations.

While environmental factors were important elements in the definition of multi-dimensional poverty, they are not included in the composite poverty measure presented in Figure 5.2 because appropriate variables were not carried by early waves of the BHPS. However, there was no fall in the child poverty associated with environmental deprivation over the period 1997 to 2003 for which data is available. Rather, it rose slightly and then fell in almost exactly the same fashion as that associated with psychological stress. This association may be coincidental, but equally it might be that parents' psychological stress is closely associated with characteristics in the local environment or that trends in both are determined by another unmeasured influence, such as housing demand.

What is clear, however, is that children are more at risk of experiencing poverty measured multi-dimensionally than are adults, but that the poverty rate among children fell faster than for adults in the dozen or so years to 2003. Moreover, it would appear that children are less exposed to material deprivation than adults in general, possibly – if other studies are taken as evidence – because parents seek to protect their children against this kind of hardship, but maybe also because certain consumer durables make parenting easier.

The risk of child poverty

Of course, studies of income poverty demonstrate that children are not all equally at risk of poverty. The same is true of multi-dimensional poverty, although the risk factors are by no means identical.

The risk of a child being poor varies according to age and household characteristics. To aid comparison, the average risk of a child being poor in 2003 – 26 per cent – is set equal to 1.0 in Table 5.1. If the risk of a child with a particular set of characteristics being poor exceeds the average, the value in the first column of Table 5.1 will be greater than 1.0. Thus, it can be seen that the risk of a child being poor is slightly more than doubled (2.04) if s/he happens to live a household in which no adult works. However, the risk of poverty is even higher among children living with lone parents, but greatest of all when the household head has a disability or long-term illness.

Comparing the first two columns of figures in Table 5.1, which record the relative risk of multi-dimensional and income poverty, is very instructive. To the extent that one accepts the argument that a multi-dimensional measure provides a more accurate index of 'true' poverty, focusing on income poverty serves significantly to distort the actual incidence of poverty and could mislead those seeking most effectively to target assistance. The income-based measure exaggerates the risk of poverty faced by a child living in a workless household and those living in social housing, compared with the more comprehensive index of multi-dimensional poverty. So, whereas the income measure prioritises worklessness as a cause or correlate of child poverty, the multi-dimensional measure underlines the importance of adult disability and somewhat downplays the risk associated with living in social housing.

Table 5.1

Risk of child poverty by household characteristic

	Relative risk 2003		Percentage change in the risk of poverty 1991–2003	
Characteristic	**Poverty Index**	**Income poverty**[1]	**Poverty Index**	**Income poverty**[1]
Living with a lone parent	2.18	2.11	34.3	36.6
Living with sick/disabled head of household	2.41	2.39	46.8	25.2
Living in council housing	1.96	2.52	40.9	11.4
Living in housing association accommodation	1.76	2.44	45.1	−5.8
Living with a workless head of household	2.04	2.88	47.2	18.0
All children	1.00	1.00	24.5	36.9

1 Equivalised household income below 60 per cent of the median before housing costs

Table 5.1 also reveals significant changes in the incidence of child poverty between 1991 and 2003 that again differ according to whether a narrow income definition of poverty or a multi-dimensional one is used. Taking an income measure, the incidence of poverty has fallen most among children living with lone parents or with a disabled head of household and least among children living in social housing. Indeed, child poverty actually rose marginally among children in housing association accommodation. This could be interpreted as a product of targeting benefits and employment support to lone parents and disabled people. The multi-dimensional measures confirm the reduction in the risk of poverty among these groups but indicate improvements of a similar, if not greater, magnitude among children in social housing attributable to factors other than increased income.

Table 5.2

Risk of child poverty by demographic characteristics

Characteristic	Relative risk 2003	
	Poverty Index	Income poverty[1]
Child aged 0–4	0.74	0.80
Child aged 5–11	1.13	1.11
Child aged 12+	0.72	1.04
1 child in household	0.99	0.66
2 children in household	0.88	0.89
3 children in household	1.10	1.29
4+ children in household	1.61	2.17
All children	1.00	1.00

1 Equivalised household income below 60% of the median before housing costs

Two demographic risk factors – age and household size – are compared in Table 5.2 and again their relative importance differs between the multi-dimensional and simple income measures. Irrespective of the measure used, primary school-aged children appear to be most at risk of poverty while pre-school-aged children are less likely than an average child to live in a poor household. However, the multi-dimensional measure suggests that secondary school-aged children are noticeably less likely than younger ones to experience poverty, while the income-based measure does not. There are subtle differences too when considering family size. Using an income measure, poverty increases with the number of children, such that children with three or more siblings are more than three times more likely to be poor than an only child. This differential proves to be much less marked when the more comprehensive measure of poverty is applied since, with this measure, the risk of a child being poor is lowest when they have a single sibling. The suggestion here, then, is that the consequences of needing to share a similar amount of income between a larger number of individuals in large families is to some extent offset when account is taken of other aspects of poverty.

Child poverty

The period 1991 to 2003 witnessed a steady and substantial decline in child poverty, measured multi-dimensionally, from over 30 per cent to a little more than 13 per cent. Much of this improvement occurred before 1999 when Tony Blair committed the Labour Government to the eradication of child poverty and, indeed, there is little evidence that the activities of government made a difference until after 2001.

As for adults, taking account of the many dimensions of poverty proves instructive. It enriches understanding of the factors most likely to be associated with child poverty – for example, adult disability increases the risk of a child experiencing poverty more than worklessness, and large family size proves to be less important than when account is taken of income alone. It is also clear that, for whatever reason, children are better protected against material deprivation than other aspects of poverty. Even so, as explained in the next chapter, household poverty has a profound negative impact on the wellbeing of children.

Notes

1   It is also possible that adults in the household have human capital resources sufficient to outweigh the poverty of the household head, although it should be noted that the methodology adopted means that the household head is assigned the appropriate equivalent household income.

2   See Appendix for a discussion of translating the Poverty Index into a relative form.

3   J Bradshaw and others, *Minimum Income Standards in Britain*, Joseph Rowntree Foundation, 2008

4   S Payne, 'Mental Health, Poverty and Social Exclusion', in C Pantazis, D Gordon and R Levitas (eds), *Poverty and Social Exclusion in Britain: the Millennium survey*, The Policy Press, 2006

Six

Poverty and childhood wellbeing

We have seen how a multi-dimensional measure of poverty can enhance our understanding of poverty and its dynamics. In this chapter we take the multi-dimensional poverty measure a stage further by exploring the relationship between it and measures of childhood wellbeing.

Anti-poverty policy in Britain, the United States and much of Europe is increasingly focused on child poverty.[1] Among the many reasons for this shift in emphasis is the evidence of the scarring effects of child poverty on adult outcomes, undermining the equality of opportunity that is meant to underpin social justice, as proposed by the influential US philosopher John Rawls.[2] However, there is growing concern in some quarters that the future-orientated emphasis on children becoming adults neglects the importance of child wellbeing in the here and now.[3] One consequence may be to misdirect policy, prioritising instrumental measures while failing directly to enhance the quality of childhood. This may curtail the chances of a child in a low-income household enjoying a 'good' childhood, an undesirable outcome in itself, but one that could also inhibit the development of personal resilience needed to break the link between child poverty and poor adult outcomes.

In Britain, the re-focusing of policy can be precisely dated to 18 March 1999 when the then Prime Minister, Tony Blair, delivered the annual Beveridge lecture and announced the goal to 'end child poverty' within 'a generation'. This important commitment was a late addition to a lecture on social justice in which Blair reasserted his meritocratic, Rawlsian view of justice, defined as equality of opportunity rather than equality of outcome. The lecture was future orientated, borrowing the sound bite from Gordon Brown, then Chancellor of the Exchequer, that while children comprised 20 per cent of the population, they were '100 per cent of the future'. Consistent with Blair's concept of social justice as 'a community where everyone has the chance to succeed', he committed the Government to breaking 'the cycle of deprivation so that children born into poverty are not condemned to social exclusion and deprivation'. The speech was followed by a blizzard of anti-child poverty policies and commitments and the publication of an annual document against which performance was to be assessed.[4] Despite lukewarm public support for the policy, political commitment to the anti-child poverty agenda has proved long-lived and has also been endorsed by leaders of the political opposition.[5]

Much of the academic literature relating to child poverty in the UK has focused on two issues. First, the identification of households where risk is greatest and, second, the so-called 'scarring' of children and the transmission of disadvantage into adulthood. With respect to the former, the risk factors are now well established. Not surprisingly, poor children are more likely to be found in low-income households, but also in: work-less households; households receiving benefits; those in rented accom-modation; lone-parent families; families with younger children; large families and ethnic minority households. From a policy perspective, the crucial issue is no longer that of identifying which children are most at risk (though the previous chapter suggests some correctives), but rather map-ping the pathways through which household poverty in all its manifesta-tions affects children and their wellbeing.

With respect to the second set of literature on scarring and trans-mission, the impact of poverty on a child's future life chances has been extensively researched and summarised.[6] Moreover, early analyses caught the attention of Gordon Brown in late 1998 and may have influ-enced the content of Blair's Beveridge lecture.[7] While this work is con-vincing, there is comparatively much less literature relating to child poverty in the here and now and its immediate impact on the life of the child. Studies suggest a complex relationship between economic hardship and child wellbeing and that the latter may mediate the effect of poverty on adult outcomes. Some British evidence points to children feeling embar-rassed and socially excluded, seeing inequality as inevitable and educa-tion futile,[8] although other work shows children being variously oblivious to their poverty, accepting of it or pestering hard for extra resources and opportunities.[9] At one extreme, children find themselves protected by par-ents and other family relationships whereas, at the other, poverty may lie at the root of abusive or ineffectual parenting.[10] Similarly, school may pro-vide a refuge and a potential means of economic escape or serve to trap low-income children in a state of under-performance.[11]

Given this somewhat confusing picture of the way that household poverty may or may not impact on the lives and wellbeing of children, there is again a need to confront head on the complexity that is real life and to use it to good effect with a view to informing policy. As it happens, variants of the same statistical modelling technique employed in Chapter 3, structural equation modelling (SEM), can be used to track the pathways by which the various dimensions of poverty affect different aspects of child wellbeing. Therefore, this chapter is devoted first of all to understanding better the ways in which children in the 'here and now' are affected by the poverty of the adults with whom they live. However, the same modelling techniques also enable us to explore the likely impact of policies designed to mediate the effects of poverty on child wellbeing.

The measurement of poverty and child wellbeing

As poverty is multi-dimensional, so too is child wellbeing. Four key dimensions are suggested from the literature that could be measured with the data available. 'Home life' is a measure of a child's relationship with her/his parents. 'Educational orientation' is a measure of how well the child is doing at school. 'Low self-worth' is a measure of the child's psychological health, while 'risky behaviour' is an attempt to measure aspects of risk-taking or anti-social behaviour.

The data used was drawn from the 2001 wave of the British Household Panel Survey (BHPS) for all households with children, after excluding the small number headed by a person aged less than 18 or over 64. The BHPS collects information on children in the sample households and, importantly, all older children (those aged between 11 and 15) complete a separate questionnaire (known as the British Youth Panel), which forms the basis for the measurement of child wellbeing presented below.

Adopting the same approach as to the multi-dimensional measure of poverty, a model of child wellbeing was constructed using the variables listed in Table 6.1 (see Figure 6.1).[12] The basic model with four dimensions was enhanced by including variables to take account of the gender and age of the child and the score of the head of household on the Poverty Index. It is important to realise that the measures of wellbeing relate only to children aged 11 to 15 since we have no data for younger children. In one sense, this is clearly a limitation. Indeed, because of the age range one might be tempted to speak of 'young people' rather than 'children'. On the other hand, the data was obtained directly from the young people themselves rather than being filtered through the perceptions of adults.

As would be expected, the four dimensions of wellbeing are inter-connected. So, as can be seen from Table 6.2, educational orientation is

Table 6.1

Measuring child wellbeing: component variables

1. **Home life** is a measure of the child's relationship with her/his parents:
- how much children talk to their parents;
- how much control parents exercise over TV;
- how much the family shares meals together.

2. **Educational orientation** is a measure of how well the child is doing at school:
- how much the child likes her/his teachers;
- whether the teachers 'get at me';
- general feelings about school;
- whether the child is doing well at school.

3. **Low self-worth** is a measure of the child's psychological health:
- whether the child feels unhappy;
- whether the child has lost sleep;
- how useless the child feels;
- how much of a failure the child feels;
- whether the child feels no good;
- the extent to which the child feels lonely;
- the extent to which the child is left out of activities.

4. **Risky behaviour** is an attempt to measure aspects of risk-taking or anti-social behaviour:
- whether the child has ever been suspended from school;
- how often the child plays truant;
- how much experience the child has with smoking cigarettes;
- whether the child vandalises property;
- whether the child has friends who use illegal drugs (there is no direct question about the respondent's own drug use).

strongly associated with home life and negatively associated with low self-worth and risky behaviour. Risky behaviour is in turn associated with low self-worth.

Consistent with previous literature, girls exhibit lower degrees of self-worth than boys, but have a better educational orientation and a greater involvement in home life (Figure 6.1). However, there is no significant difference between girls and boys with respect to risky behaviour. On the other hand, as children get older their propensity to engage in risky behaviour increases, while their attachment to home life and their commitment to education tend to diminish.

Figure 6.1

A basic model of child wellbeing (arrows show significant impacts)

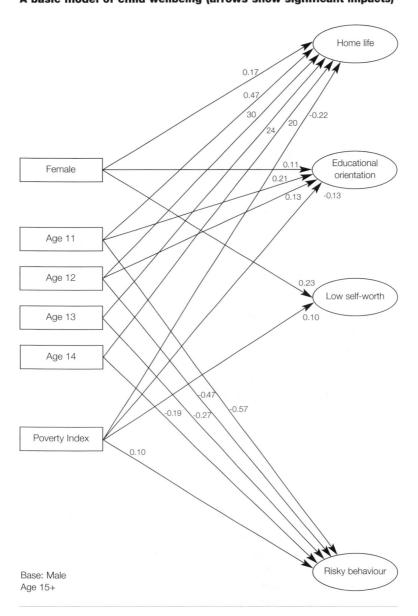

Base: Male
Age 15+

Table 6.2

Correlations between the dimensions of child wellbeing

	Home life	Educational orientation	Low self-worth
Educational orientation	+0.54		
Low self-worth	−0.18	−0.36	
Risky behaviour	−0.63	−0.54	+0.22

However, the most striking finding is that poverty (measured by the composite multi-dimensional Poverty Index) has a highly significant and detrimental effect on *all four dimensions* of child wellbeing: contributing to low self-worth and risky behaviour while detracting from educational orientation and engagement in home life. Nonetheless, the impact of poverty on each dimension of wellbeing is not uniform. Rather, the strongest negative effect appears to be on home life, followed by that on educational orientation. The impact on low self-worth and risky behaviour is less marked, but still statistically significant.

If, as we contend, poverty is multi-dimensional, one might expect that the various dimensions of household poverty have a differential effect on child wellbeing. This turns out to be the case. Since the Poverty Index is a weighted sum of six sub-indices, it proved possible to establish which dimensions of household poverty have a statistically significant impact on child wellbeing (Figure 6.2). It emerges that financial strain affects all four dimensions of child wellbeing, but that material deprivation is associated with just two, increasing risky behaviour and negatively affecting home life. The environment dimension of poverty, relating both to poor housing conditions and a deprived neighbourhood, is associated with reduced quality of home life, low self-worth and risky behaviour. However, the social isolation of the head of household, sometimes interpreted as a measure of social capital, has no bearing on any of the four indicators of child wellbeing.

It is unlikely that all children living in poor families will be affected by poverty in the same way. We know, for example, that parents often go out of their way to protect children from the financial and social consequences of poverty and that some parents may, for a variety of reasons, be in a better position than others to do this. Within the severe constraints imposed by available data, an attempt was made to investigate these mediating influences (summarised in Table 6.3). The effect of household composition was explored by including a variable indicating

Figure 6.2

How different aspects of poverty impact on aspects of wellbeing

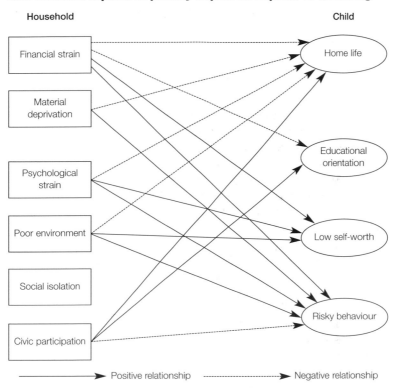

whether the household was headed by a single adult and variables representing the number of children in different age categories. Likewise, the possible influence of the educational and employment and employment status of the head of household was considered, as was the level of income available.

The results show that the children in single-adult households are less likely than others to eat or talk with their parent or to have their access to television monitored – variables that relate to the home life dimension. They are also more likely to engage in risky behaviour, but do not differ from other children in terms of educational orientation or sense of self-worth. In certain respects, therefore, the wellbeing of children in lone-parent households may be compromised. This may possibly be because,

Table 6.3

Effects of various factors on child wellbeing with various controls in addition to age and gender of the child

	Household composition	Education of head	Employment status of head	Household income
Significant impact on:				
Home life	−0.11 (Single adult household)	+0.23 (Higher education)	−0.11 (Unemployed) −0.11 (Non-employed)	+0.16
Educational orientation	ns	+0.15 (Higher education)	−0.10 (Non-employed)	+0.11
Low self-worth	ns	ns	+0.07* (Non-employed)	ns
Risky behaviour	+0.09 (Single adult household)	ns	+0.08 (Unemployed) +0.09 (Non-employed)	−0.09*

ns = not statistically significant
* = marginally significant at 5% level

with just one adult, the total volume of care available is less in lone-parent households. Certainly, the modelling indicated that the lower incomes of lone-parent families do not account for the observed differences in child wellbeing. The presence of other children or siblings also appears to have no effect on children's wellbeing.

The impact of poverty on child wellbeing seems to be influenced by the employment status of the household head, but in complex ways. Where the household head is unemployed, children are more prone to engage in risky behaviour and to have a poor home life. On the other hand, their educational attachment is unaffected as is their sense of self-worth. Children brought up in households in which the head is economically inactive, which would include people who are disabled and for other reasons not required to look for work, appear to be somewhat more adversely affected in that they are disadvantaged on all four dimensions of wellbeing. This difference may reflect the impact of long-term poverty on children since this is more likely to occur among households headed by a person who is economically inactive, as unemployment is more typically intermittent, and interspersed with periods of relatively greater prosperity.

One might anticipate children of more educated parents would have a competitive advantage over other children, certainly in terms of educational orientation and possibly in terms quality of home life. The evidence is that this is the case for children in households where the head has received higher education, meaning the negative effects of poverty on children are mediated on these two dimensions of wellbeing. However, lower levels of parental education do not appear sufficient to prevent the corrosive effect of poverty on child wellbeing, and even a higher level education fails to inoculate children against the increased risk of low self-esteem and of engaging in risky behaviour associated with living in poverty.

To conclude, poverty not only scars children in the long term, as demonstrated by earlier research, it also has negative consequences for children in the immediate present. Moreover, the different dimensions of poverty affect children in varying ways. Furthermore, the impact of poverty on a child's mental state is greater than the effect of low income alone, significantly lowering her/his sense of self-worth, as well as the other dimensions of wellbeing, in a way that income does not (Table 6.3). All this points to the importance of relying on other policies as well as on cash benefits to tackle the problem of child poverty and raises the possibility that anti-poverty policies might be better targeted on particular aspects of poverty in order to maximise their effect on child wellbeing.

Potential policy implications of the model

In Britain, the Government's determined assault on poverty has employed a wide range of policy instruments. These have included a strong emphasis on help for families, including lone parents in particular, through the tax credit and benefit system and a range of measures to break the inter-generational inheritance of poverty, ranging from investment in health and schools to the provision of early years education, investment in deprived communities and parenting support. However, the central thrust of policy has been to encourage workless parents into employment while paying somewhat less attention to other aspects of a child's environment. But, while child poverty has fallen, improvements have stubbornly been below target and specific policies, such as the New Deal for Lone Parents designed to encourage lone parents to take up employment, have sometimes failed to provide the secure, well-paid employment necessary to lift families out of poverty.[13]

Moreover, the indicators the Government has chosen to use to target policy and to measure its effectiveness (income and deprivation) have proved problematic. Income measures show wide fluctuations over time within households while low income, as we have shown, does not always correlate very well with deprivation or with the other dimensions of poverty which the government has largely overlooked. While the multi-faceted nature of poverty has been acknowledged, its cumulative character has hardly registered because of the use of a multiplicity of separate indicators.

In a context in which the Government seeks new policy instruments in order to renew its commitment to reduce or eradicate child poverty, the foregoing analysis points to the possibility that policies could, in principle, be targeted on different aspects of household poverty to the benefit of the current generation of children. For example, the analysis suggests that improving the environment of children – both within and outside the household – may well have a greater overall impact on wellbeing than improving material deprivation. Equally, if the goal is to enhance educational performance, then alleviating financial strain and encouraging civic participation of parents may be important strategies since these appear to mediate the effects of poverty on child wellbeing. On the other hand, the social isolation of the head of household, often taken as a measure of social capital, seems to have little bearing on any of the four indicators of child wellbeing.

The methodology presented above can be further exploited to explore the likely impact on child wellbeing of policy options that succeed in tackling the various dimensions of household poverty. By simulating improvements of the various dimensions of poverty, it is possible to assess the potential effect of successfully targeted policies on the child wellbeing scores generated for the Youth Panel. Tables 6.4 and 6.5 present the results of such simulations, showing the predicted consequences for child wellbeing of changing the different components of household poverty in the following manner:

- moving from a completely materially deprived to a fully-equipped household;
- moving from a relatively frequent level of deprivation to no deprivation (frequent deprivation refers to a household that does not have: a PC, dishwasher, dryer, car, and cable/satellite TV, and that cannot afford

holidays once a year, to replace worn furniture or to feed visitors once
a month);
- moving from the most intense financial hardship to none;
- moving from the worst housing to having no housing problems;
- moving from the worst kind of neighbourhood to one which has no
problems;
- finally, a combined effect of improved housing and neighbourhood
change (that is, our total environmental dimension).

In order to ensure comparability, changes in each dimension of child wellbeing are expressed as a percentage of a standard deviation, a common
metric like a universal thermometer.

The aspect of child wellbeing that shows most potential improvement as a result of reductions in poverty is family life (Table 6.4). Significant
improvements on family life could be achieved by tackling any of the
dimensions of child poverty, although by far the largest impact might
come from relieving financial pressure on families. Although small changes
in material deprivation have quite large effects on a child's educational orientation (possibly due to an improved infrastructure for learning within the
household), they have only limited impact on family life. Simultaneously
tackling the various dimensions of poverty could bring cumulative benefits. So, the analysis suggests that improving both housing and neighbourhood conditions could have a marked influence on all four dimensions of
child wellbeing. The combined effect is to increase the quality of home life
by 41 per cent of a standard deviation and educational attachment by 26
per cent, while reducing risky behaviour and low self-esteem by 17 per
cent and 15 per cent of a standard deviation respectively.

Alleviating financial pressure would improve the quality of home life
by a very substantial 62 per cent of a standard deviation and diminish risky
behaviour by 25 per cent of a standard deviation. However, it is important
to recognise that alleviating financial pressure is more than just increasing
income, though this is critically important to it. When income alone is
increased and other aspects of financial pressure are held constant, the
impact on child wellbeing is much reduced (Table 6.5). Even lifting households with half median incomes up to the median only yields a 21 per cent
standard deviation increase in the quality of a child's home life and an 8
per cent standard deviation reduction in risky behaviour. The logic, therefore, is that tackling poverty in the round is necessary to maximise the
benefits for children and that solely addressing income poverty is an inadequate response to the social problem represented by poverty. Again, this

Table 6.4

Impact of various household changes on child wellbeing after controlling for gender and age (numbers refer to changes in the % of a standard deviation)

Dimension	Full deprivation to no deprivation	Common deprivation to no deprivation	Intense financial pressure to no financial pressure	Bad housing to best housing	Bad neighbourhood to best neighbourhood	Total environmental effect
Home life	+26%	+3%	+62%	+23%	+18%	+41%
Educational orientation	+15%	+8%	+39%	+15%	+11%	+26%
Low self-worth	–9%	–1%	–24%	–9%	–6%	–15%
Risky behaviour	–8%	–1%	–25%	–8%	–8%	–17%

Table 6.5

Impact of household income changes on child wellbeing after controlling for gender and age (numbers refer to change in the % of a standard deviation)

Dimension	50% median to median income	60% median to median income	70% median to median income	80% median to median income	90% median to median Income
Home life	+21%	+16%	+11%	+8%	+3%
Educational orientation	+15%	+11%	+9%	+4%	+2%
Low self-worth	–9%	–3%	–3%	0%	0%
Risky behaviour	–8%	–8%	–4%	–4%	0%

underlines the importance of using multi-dimensional poverty indicators in any serious analysis.

Finally, we can use a similar methodology to investigate the impact of changing employment status and household composition on child wellbeing: two matters at the heart of current debates about addressing child poverty (Table 6.6) The analysis indicates that changing the status of a household head from employment to unemployment has substantial negative effects on a child's home life, risky behaviour and educational orientation – effects which, in the symmetrical world of cross-sectional modelling, could be reversed by policies that successfully help unemployed people enter work. The implication, therefore, is that successful work activation programmes targeted at unemployed people could also have beneficial effects for the children of those who successfully secure employment.

However, the differential effects of changing status from employment to unemployment or to non-employment suggest that the current UK policy of extending the coverage of such schemes to the economically inactive, including lone parents and disabled people, could have a noticeably more limited positive effect. Certainly, the impact of the difference between employment and non-employment on home life and engagement in risky behaviour is much less than that associated with the difference between employment and unemployment. On the other hand, policies targeted at the economically inactive might, if successful, additionally contribute to a child's sense of worth, something that the modelling predicts is unlikely to happen when an unemployed person gets a job. This, in turn, could suggest that young people see job search as a mani-

---

Table 6.6

Impact of moving from various household states on child wellbeing after controlling for gender and age (numbers refer to change in the % of a standard deviation)

	Loss of an adult from the household	Becoming a one-parent household	Household head moves from employed to unemployed	Household head moves from employed to non-employed
Home life	−1%	−35%	−62%	−34%
Educational orientation	+6%	−11%	−38%	−31%
Low self-worth	−2%	+12%	−1%	+19%
Risky behaviour	+3%	+23%	+38%	+23%

festation of an adult's positive work ethic (and not just employment) and gain emotional sustenance from it.

The modelling indicates that a reduction in the number of adults in a household has little effect on child wellbeing, but that the difference between a multiple adult and a lone-parent household is marked. The largest detrimental effect associated with a child living with a lone parent is on home life (reducing it by 35 per cent of a standard deviation), but there are also associated increases in risky behaviour and, to a lesser extent, increases in low self-worth and decreases in educational orientation in lone-parent households. This finding reflects the earlier observation that household structure is important in mediating the impact of the various dimensions of poverty on child wellbeing. It also chimes well with the policy attention being given by the British Conservative opposition to ways of supporting the traditional two-parent nuclear family. Whether it would prove possible to reverse the demographic momentum towards cohabitation and lone parenthood is a moot point, although there is little evidence that the sustained attempts to do so in the United States have proved very effective.[14] Thought, nevertheless, needs to be given to policies that would counteract the apparent negative consequences of growing up in a lone-parent family. Our analysis suggests that strategies that rely on increased income alone and ignore the role of other supports are unlikely to prove to be successful.

Conclusions

While not wishing to ignore the importance of research demonstrating that poverty can scar children for life, attention has been drawn to the complementary need to focus on the effects of poverty on children in the here and now. The analysis shows that, other things being equal, children who are poor are more likely than others to report having a difficult home life, to have negative attitudes towards school, to feel isolated and anxious and to engage in anti-social and risky behaviour. Perhaps even more importantly, the research demonstrates that household poverty comprises different dimensions and that each has different effects on the four aspects of child wellbeing that have been captured with the data available.

For example, it seems clear that where adults are not succeeding well in making ends meet, this has significant effects on all aspects of a child's wellbeing. Moreover, the associated psychological problems that many adults experience when poor independently impact on a child's mental wellbeing, their chance of engaging in risky behaviour and, perhaps not surprisingly, on their reports of the quality of their home life. Likewise, poor housing and unsatisfactory local environments exert their toll. It is clearly important, therefore, to recognise that poverty adds significantly to pressures in children's lives and directly diminishes the experience of childhood. It also seems likely that differentiated policy instruments will be required to ameliorate the impact of different dimensions of poverty on each element of child wellbeing.

Notes

1 European Union, *Child Poverty and Well-Being in the EU: current status and way forward*, European Commission, Directorate-General for Employment, Social Affairs and Equal Opportunities, 2008; HM Treasury, *Ending Child Poverty: everybody's business*, HM Treasury, The Stationery Office, 2008; Commission for Economic Opportunity, 'Increasing Opportunity and Reducing Poverty in New York City', The New York City Commission for Economic Opportunity Report to Mayor Michael R Bloomberg, 2006

2 J Rawls, *A Theory of Justice*, Harvard University Press, 1971

3 L Sutton, 'A Child's Eye View', *Poverty* 126 (Winter), 2007, pp8-11; T Ridge, *Childhood Poverty and Social Exclusion*, The Policy Press, 2002

4 J Hills and K Stewart (eds), *A More Equal Society? New Labour, poverty, inequality and exclusion*, The Policy Press, 2005; Department for Work and Pensions, *Opportunity for All: indicators update 2007*, Department for Work and Pensions, 2007

5 S Cross and P Golding, 'A Poor Press? Media reception of the Beveridge lecture', in R Walker (ed), *Ending Child Poverty: popular welfare for the 21st Century*, The Policy Press, 1999, pp121-38; D Cameron, 'Together We Can End Poverty', Speech given in London on 28 April 2008, available at www.youtube.com/watch?v=o1PDBynvnC4

6 HM Treasury, *Ending Child Poverty: everybody's business*, HM Treasury, The Stationery Office, 2008; Children's Defense Fund, *Child Poverty in America*, Children's Defense Fund, 2007; E Such and R Walker, 'Falling Behind? Research on transmitted deprivation', *Benefits* 10(3), 2002, pp185-92

7 A Lee and J Hills, *New Cycles of Disadvantage? Report of a conference organised by CASE on behalf of ESRC for HM Treasury*, CASE Report 1, Centre for the Analysis of Social Exclusion, London School of Economics,1998

8 P Attree, 'The Social Costs of Child Poverty: a systematic review of the qualitative evidence', *Children and Society* 20(1), 2006, pp54-66; S O'Neill, *The Cost of Education*, End Child Poverty Network Cymru, 2006

9   S Fortier, 'On Being a Poor Child in America: views of poverty from 7–12-year-olds', *Journal of Children and Poverty* 12(2), 2006, pp113-28; S Middleton, K Ashworth and I Braithwaite, *Small Fortunes: spending on children, childhood poverty and parental sacrifice*, Joseph Rowntree Foundation, 1997

10   S Bartlett, 'No Place to Play: implications for the interaction of parents and children', *Journal of Children and Poverty* 3(1), 1997, pp37-48; R Barth, J Wildfire and R Green, 'Placement into Foster Care and the Interplay of Urbanicity, Child Behavior Problems and Poverty', *American Journal of Orthopsychiatry* 76(3), 2006, pp358-66; I Katz, J Corlyon, V La Placa and S Hunter, *The Relationship between Parenting and Poverty*, Joseph Rowntree Foundation, 2007

11   G Horgan, *The Impact of Poverty on Young Children's Experience of School*, Joseph Rowntree Foundation, 2007; G Ansalone, 'Schooling, Tracking and Inequality', *Journal of Children and Poverty* 7(1), 2001, pp33-47

12   See M Tomlinson, R Walker and G Williams, 'The Relationship Between Poverty and Child Well-being in Great Britain', *Barnett Papers in Social Research* 3, Department of Social Policy and Social Work, University of Oxford, 2008, for a more detailed and technical discussion of the model.

13   A Yeo, *Experience of Work and Job Retention Among Lone Parents: an evidence review*, DWP Working Paper 37, Corporate Document Services, 2007

14   P Birch, S Weed and J Olsen, 'Assessing the Impact of Community Marriage Policies on County Divorce Rates', *Family Relations* 53(5), 2004, pp495-503; C Trenholm, B Devaney, K Fortson, L Quay, J Wheeler and M Clark, *Impacts of Four Title V, Section 510 Abstinence Education Programs, Final Report*, Mathematica Policy Research, 2007

Seven

Multi-dimensional poverty and policy

We began this book by acknowledging that poverty is thankfully now high on the political agenda. The importance attached to child poverty and the progress made in tackling the poverty of families with children are undisputed, although much more still needs to be done if Blair's bold target to eradicate child poverty is to be achieved. Moreover, writing in a world that is being buffeted by financial storms with rising unemployment and a housing market in crisis, the future is very uncertain.[1] Nevertheless, the Government appears to be still committed to meeting its targets. At the 2008 Labour Party conference, Prime Minister Gordon Brown proclaimed that child poverty 'demeans Britain' and reaffirmed his party's pledge to halve child poverty by 2010, and ultimately to end it completely,[2] despite the fact that child poverty is now on the rise again.

The Conservatives – who before the so-called 'credit crunch' and the ensuing crisis looked set to take power after the next general election – are also committed to tackling poverty. Notions of poverty, fairness and the gap between rich and poor have now become part of the lexicon of the official opposition, although their emphasis in terms of solutions is often slightly different. This is a far cry from the days of Thatcherism, when poverty was an unspoken word and so-called 'genuine' poverty had supposedly all but been eradicated. In 2006, Oliver Letwin committed the Conservatives to upholding Labour's targets on child poverty, but it remains to be seen whether this commitment will make its way into the manifesto at the next general election.[3]

Complexity

Poverty is still often measured in terms of a lack of income. This is not only a form of simple shorthand for there is a strong underlying historical rationale as noted in Chapter 2. In the nineteenth century, the interest of social reformers in measuring poverty was based on moral rather than scientific values in that they wanted to mobilise support for the cause by the most direct route possible. This goal demanded that they demonstrate that poverty was due to a person's lack of resources rather than to reckless expenditure, hence their focus was on establishing how much income poor people had in relation to the income required to attain a decent standard of living.

However, to focus only on income poverty is to misunderstand the true multi-faceted nature of poverty and the complexity of poor people's lives. It can also lead to wrong conclusions about the incidence, causes and consequences of poverty as we have repeatedly demonstrated throughout this book. Such misconceptions can, in turn, result in poorly targeted and ineffectual policies. Even if income poverty is reduced within a household, this does not immediately lead to a cessation of the other problems associated with limited financial resources. It takes time after a prolonged period of low income to replace worn-out durables and recover from material deprivation, to overcome low self-esteem and improve the immediate home environment. For a substantial period, the household is also likely to remain vulnerable to repeated spells of financial hardship.

The complexity of poverty is an enduring problem for policy makers. The diversity of poverty experienced by different segments of the population makes simple solutions hard to find. We have sought to understand the relative weight of different dimensions of poverty using statistical techniques that can cope with this complexity and by exploring detailed and comprehensive longitudinal data. In this way, we have begun to be able to isolate those dimensions of poverty that are the most salient for the individuals and families affected and to explore the interrelations between these different aspects of poverty over quite a long period of time. The sophisticated statistical techniques employed allow us to measure complex and inherently difficult to observe phenomena associated with being poor and help us to separate the wheat from the chaff in terms of what is relevant and what is not. The same techniques could be used to assist in the design and targeting of policy.

Our approach has enabled us to isolate various dimensions of the problem: namely financial strain, material deprivation, social isolation, civic participation, the environment and the psychological strain associated with poverty. Some of these dimensions are more tied up with each other than others. For example, not surprisingly, there was a strong association between financial strain and material deprivation (but they still emerged as separate dimensions in their own right). The approach also validated the notion that there is an ordered pyramid of concepts of increasing importance when seeking to measure and better understand poverty. Nevertheless, many dimensions play a role in shaping the overall experience of poverty and the relative strength of these dimensions changes over time.

The summary measures of poverty that combine the various dimensions into a single index also have several advantages over other indicators in common use. It has previously proved nigh on impossible to devise multi-dimensional measures that are stable over time and which thereby facilitate accurate measurement of trends in the poverty rate. This is a fundamental requirement if the effects of anti-poverty programmes are to be assessed. The poverty indices we devised overcome many of measurement problems of other approaches and do not suffer wide fluctuations from one year to the next. Moreover, our approach is a significant advance on the various methods used up to now which cannot adequately cope with the situation where a person might appear poor on one index and not on another. It is, though, limited by available data appertaining to the various dimensions of poverty.

The substantive findings demonstrate that poverty, measured as a multi-dimensional concept, fell throughout the 1990s and early 2000s without a marked turning point associated with the election of the New Labour Government in 1997.[4] This was true of both absolute and relative measures. The decline was mainly driven by falls in financial stress, but also by reduced material deprivation particularly during the early 1990s, a time when unemployment, inflation and interest rates were falling and remained at historically low levels.

In terms of the relative importance of the dimensions under consideration, the models revealed the dominating importance of financial pressure brought about by the combination of financial stress (ie, difficulty in coping) and material deprivation. Nevertheless, poverty was also indexed and experienced as a manifestation of psychological strain (that changed little over the period) and reflected environmental factors such as bad housing and poor neighbourhoods. It was perhaps surprising that social isolation and civic participation (both related in one way or another to social exclusion) have a much less marked impact on the multi-dimensional poverty measures. It also suggests that strategies that prioritise the building of social capital may not, by themselves, achieve all that is sometimes expected of them. That said, measures of both these dimensions of poverty could be significantly improved if different questions were added to the British Household Panel Survey (to be integrated in the new UK Household Longitudinal Study, 'Understanding Society').

The analysis presented in Chapter 3 confirmed the now widely observed finding that income is only weakly associated with other manifestations of poverty[5] and underlines the need to take a multi-dimensional approach seriously in order to develop the tools necessary for the accurate measurement of poverty and related phenomena. The pyramid of concepts proved to be a useful starting point when coupled with the more advanced statistical techniques becoming available.

Poverty dynamics, children and families

The long-term dynamics of poverty were analysed in detail in Chapter 4, again using a multi-dimensional approach. The groups most at long-term risk of experiencing poverty proved to include the following groups: single people, lone parents, those who are not working, those working in low-skilled and/or part-time jobs, fragmented households, women and minority ethnic groups. While employment certainly reduces poverty, lone-parent families in particular were found still to be prone to poverty, even if they managed to secure paid employment. Furthermore, two-parent families that split as a consequence of relationship breakdown were similarly at high risk of poverty affecting both partners in the relationship – although women proved to suffer more than men after other characteristics had been taken into consideration.

Other research has shown that poverty in childhood can have a profound effect on life chances and on social and economic outcomes in adulthood. Indeed, the current emphasis that the Government places on reducing child poverty is sometimes narrowly conceived in terms of a financial logic that attempts to calculate the costs to future generations of the transmission of bad outcomes from one generation to the next. Attention has been drawn in Chapters 5 and 6 to the complementary need to focus on the effects of poverty on children and young people in the present. Taking the multi-dimensional analysis a stage further, we demonstrated that children and young people, aged 11 to 15, who are poor are likely to have an inferior quality of life, lower wellbeing, than their contemporaries. We also showed how different dimensions of household poverty have diverse impacts on various aspects of child wellbeing. As discussed later in this chapter, these statistical relationships could be used to more effectively direct policy orientated at alleviating the impact of poverty on families with children in the here and now.

In addition to the effects of low income on children in families, we demonstrated the additional burdens imposed on them by the psychological strain exhibited by parents under financial pressure, and by living in poor housing and deprived neighbourhoods in particular. There was even evidence that the psychological stress of parents can find expression in the lower self-esteem reported by their children. It would seem clear, therefore, that the effects of child poverty that manifest themselves in later life could have their roots in dimensions of poverty that can be isolated and therefore addressed in the present, thereby avoiding the long-term 'scarring' attributable to poverty.

Policy

A wide array of policy tools has been deployed by the Labour Government since 1997 in its fight against poverty and, latterly, child poverty. Many have been employed to tackle worklessness – households in which no one is employed – which is seen as a major cause of poverty. Welfare-to-work schemes, introduced under the banner of the 'New Deal', targeted an increasing number of groups ranging from young people, to people aged 25+, aged 50+, lone parents and disabled people. Jobcentre Plus combined job centres, benefit agencies and employment services under one roof in an attempt to provide finely tuned programmes and assistance for the unemployed. More recently, the employment and support allowance has been introduced, lessening the distinction between disabled and other people of working age, while the Flexible New Deal, to be introduced in 2009, seeks to consolidate the various welfare-to-work schemes and to increase further the role played by private sector organisations in the delivery of services. Increased employment-orientated conditionality and sanctions have been applied across a larger proportion of the working-age benefit recipient population.

Alongside welfare to work, there have been various initiatives 'to make work pay' and, hence, to tackle financial disincentives thought to deter people on benefits from seeking employment, and also to address in-work poverty. Foremost among them have been the introduction of a minimum wage, development of the tax credit system and repeated reductions in income tax. These direct policies have been coupled with far-reaching investments in health and education, as well as targeted investment for run-down communities and extra help for parents.

Children's services, such as Sure Start and the rolling out of free childcare for very young children, were implemented as part of the National Childcare Strategy, with guaranteed school places provided for four-year-olds instead of the usual mandatory starting age of five. Such policies were not only seen as better for children, but as also enabling mothers to enter, or re-enter, the labour market and gain access to training.

Adult poverty

These measures no doubt contributed to rising employment rates and falling poverty, but recently, ahead of the global financial crisis, child poverty began to rise again and the interim child poverty reduction targets look very vulnerable against the prospect of increasing unemployment. Moreover, as is evident from our analysis, poverty rates, measured as a multidimensional concept, were already falling before Labour came to power in 1997, suggesting that the improvements were not solely due to new policies. Furthermore, our evidence suggests that there are dangers in policies that overemphasise employment as the principal antidote to poverty. While paid work is important, quality employment is even more important; not all kinds of work are sufficient to protect families and children from long-term poverty. Low-skilled employment may be of benefit only if it turns out to be stable and to provide a stepping stone to improved long-term prospects, further advancement or training. Lone parents, in particular, need decent jobs to lift them out of poverty and to hold them there. New research currently underway by the authors suggests that there is a significant gain from skills-based training, both on and off the job, providing long-term protection from poverty facilitated by improved career prospects. General training appears to have less of an impact unless it is tied to an employer. Thus, a policy that would really help lone parents back to work would have to provide quite specific, rather than general, training and help with appropriate job placement – preferably with a family-friendly employer.[6]

Government is already responding to fears of rising unemployment linked to the prospect of global recession with measures to help meet mortgage costs and to provide rapid access to assistance with job search. If job layoffs turn into a deluge of redundancies, the temptation may be to increase conditionality so as to encourage jobseekers to take 'any job', overlooking the above findings that only quality jobs offer sustained protection against poverty.

A deep recession might also result in the Government neglecting the socio-demographic triggers that precipitate long or repeated spells of poverty. Foremost among them are separation and divorce, the effects of which are not only dramatic in the immediate aftermath, but also in the longer term. Indeed, the effect of separation on a couple (whether married or co-habiting) in terms of increasing risk of poverty was much greater than for any of the other triggers that we were able to investigate, including job loss. This was true of both men and women, although the impact was worse for the latter. If any policy lessons are to be drawn from this finding beyond the potential importance of reconciliation services, it would be the need for increased assistance to couples who have recently separated, especially when children are involved.

Part of the reason that women are so much more vulnerable to poverty than men following separation is their weak position in the labour market, given continuing wage discrimination and the existence of 'glass ceilings' that limit progress and possibly lessen ambition. The analysis revealed strong gender effects that left women more susceptible to poverty than men over long periods. Similarly, powerful effects were found for ethnicity, despite less than perfect measurement, with non-whites of both genders being noticeably more at risk of poverty long term than their white counterparts. Although it is already widely appreciated by policy makers that women and certain ethnic groups are particularly likely to be poor, the fact that they are more likely to remain poor, or at risk of poverty, for long periods deserves more recognition that it has hitherto achieved. This might be especially so if the current economic downturn is sustained.

However, perhaps the most important policy lesson of all is that poverty is more complex than simple income measures suggest. Income, as noted above, is not that strongly related to other measures of poverty and increasing income alone will not eradicate poverty. Likewise, social isolation and civic participation make a statistically significant, though comparatively limited, contribution to the overall poverty score, which might suggest a real distinction between poverty and social exclusion (although measurement issues make this more of a hypothesis than an assertion based on evidence). What is clear, however, is that in the same way that it is increasingly recognised that a personalised, multi-faceted service is required to assist jobseekers successfully into employment, so a similar approach needs to be applied to poverty. Poverty is simultaneously one thing and many and, as a consequence, likely to be susceptible only to a holistic policy response. This is consistent with the across-government drive to eradicate poverty and, to the extent that poverty is viewed as part of the European concept of social inclusion, with the obligations on Britain under the European Commission Lisbon Strategy to 'mainstream' social inclusion – ie, to take it into account in all aspects of policy making. However, the real challenge is to ensure that such comprehensive, joined-up thinking reaches the fingertips of organisations where bureaucracy both touches and helps to shape the lives of poor people.

Child poverty

Adult poverty and changes in adult circumstances have been shown in Chapter 6 to have immediate effects on the wellbeing of older children and young people that could well help to explain the negative long-term effects of poverty on child outcomes. Moreover, it has been possible to simulate the effects of tackling the various dimensions of household poverty on child wellbeing with striking results. For example, it would appear that the quality of a child's home life is particularly sensitive to almost all aspects of poverty and that, therefore, policies which succeed in reducing the financial strain experienced by parents, lessen material deprivation, enhance the quality of the local environment and increase civic participation might simultaneously improve the home life of children. A further implication is that any increase in poverty associated with recession is also likely to have immediate effects on child wellbeing and, if poverty is lengthy, increasing vulnerability to disadvantage later in life.

The modelling that we presented in Chapter 6 suggested that all four dimensions of the child's wellbeing – relationships at home, educational attachment, risky behaviour and self-esteem – were closely related to housing and neighbourhood conditions. It is at least possible, therefore, that regenerating poor neighbourhoods and improving housing could have a marked impact on children's overall wellbeing, including educational performance and reduced involvement in crime and anti-social behaviour, goals that have not in the past been much associated with urban regeneration policy. To the extent any growth in unemployment is sustained and geographically concentrated, it could deleteriously affect child wellbeing through environmental factors as well as via falls in household income.

While tackling environmental factors could protect and benefit children, the biggest single effect would seem to be achieved by alleviating financial pressures on parents. However, it is again important to recognise that alleviating financial pressure is not simply a matter of increasing income. When income changes alone were factored into the statistical models, the impact was somewhat diminished, which serves to emphasise the advantages of multi-dimensional indicators and the limitations of one-track policies. The fundamental policy logic that flows from these findings is that tackling poverty along all its dimensions is necessary to maximise the benefits for children. This poses significant challenges for policymakers, not least at a time of public expenditure constraint. It is necessary, therefore, not just to tackle poverty through the tax and benefits system, but also to adopt a much more systemic approach that simultaneously addresses several complex and interrelated processes by which different aspects of poverty impact on the lives of children. Equally, there could be unexpected benefits from such a co-ordinated response, as illustrated by the possible beneficial effects of urban regeneration on child wellbeing.

The triggers that increase the likelihood of poverty among adults perhaps, not surprisingly, generally also have negative effects on the wellbeing of children. It might be possible, therefore, to enhance child wellbeing by means of proactive strategies that help to prevent such events or to ameliorate their consequences. The modelling indicated that the unemployment of a parent had substantial negative effects on a child's home life, educational orientation and propensity to engage in risky behaviour. An important by-product of policies that help unemployed people enter work might be to reverse these effects for children. Thus, successful work activation programmes targeted on the unemployed might not only have beneficial effects for adults but also for the children of those who successfully secure employment. However, at the risk of repetition, it will be recalled that our analysis also suggested that the important achievement is not work itself, not even well-paid work, but employment with prospects that lead to longer-term stability.

The modelling also lent qualified support to policies that assist people outside the labour market to find employment, lone parents receiving income support and people receiving incapacity benefit (or employment and support allowance). Again, the children of people making the transition into employment are likely themselves to benefit through enhanced wellbeing. However, the indirect impact on child wellbeing of successful welfare-to-work policies targeted at the economically inactive are likely to be different from, and less than, those aimed at the unemployed. The modelling suggests that policies that assist the economically inactive may serve to enhance the self-esteem of participants' children – possibly because employment is so highly valued socially – but are less likely than policies that tackle unemployment to affect the other dimensions of child wellbeing. Also, of course, it is difficult to say how far engaging lone parents in employment would, in reality, overcome the loss in child wellbeing associated with being brought up in a lone-parent family, ranging from a less satisfactory home life to lower self-esteem and an increase in risky behaviour. The American evidence is that it certainly helps, although some negative consequences have been reported for teenage children.[7] What again is clear is that neither income nor employment is likely to be a sufficient mechanism on its own to eradicate poverty or to reduce significantly its detrimental impact on child wellbeing.

Instead, the policy logic that follows from the child-focussed analysis of Chapter 6 is the requirement for a well-rounded strategy that would attempt to counteract the many processes by which poverty affects child wellbeing. The analysis supports elements in the Government's current strategy. It suggests, for example, that children may suffer less from the effects of poverty if their parents are in work. However, this is only part of the story, for the type of work and the prospects associated with the work are more important than is usually recognised. Moreover, children in households where adults are experiencing financial stress suffer badly and employment does not always succeed in lifting families clear of income poverty or in placing them on an even financial keel. In the case of the children of lone parents, the analysis builds a strong case for extra support, irrespective of whether the parent is employed or not.

The logic that underpins the kind of analysis begun in this book calls for a more radical shift in policy thinking than might be immediately apparent from the preceding paragraph. It points to a redefinition in the nature of the policy problem. Rather than focusing on poverty because it scars children's futures, it encourages us to recognise that poverty also blights childhood. Moreover, because poverty is multi-dimensional and multi-faceted, it deleteriously affects childhood in multiple ways, ways that it is increasingly possible to research and hence to respond to in policy terms. Even in a recession, existing policies to raise family incomes and promote adult employment should be accompanied by a range of new policies, some of which might need to be explicitly child-focused. Addressing the different dimensions of poverty is likely to have a range of beneficial effects on children. For example, our analysis suggests that implementing a more comprehensive and coherent neighbourhood regeneration policy could improve all aspects of child wellbeing. Furthermore, if such a policy were able to incorporate significant elements of local participation, this might be doubly effective since the analysis found that civic participation by parents had a surprisingly high impact on child wellbeing. The analysis also points to the need to explore ways in which the psychological strain of adults in poor households can be alleviated – as this negatively affects the mental wellbeing of the children, and undermines home life.

Of course, no research is definitive and we plan to exploit more fully the longitudinal potential of the British Household Panel Survey by observing the consequences of actual changes in family circumstances and transitions on the wellbeing of children expressed within a multi-dimensional framework. We need also to look more closely at the factors that protect some children against the most pernicious consequences of poverty. Nevertheless, it is to be hoped that research such as that presented above, which focuses on the immediate effects of poverty, will further enthuse governments to continue to pursue the goal of eradicating child poverty. The clear message is that the social gains from this strategy do not all lie in the future. Rather, the immediate benefit is that 3.9 million children in Britain could potentially enjoy a childhood freed from the familial stress, academic failure, anxiety and social isolation that so often accompanies poverty.

Notes

1   How the poverty threshold values will be affected by the current economic turmoil could actually help the government meet its targets. If the highest income earners are disproportionately affected the thresholds could come down, thus reducing relative poverty headcounts.

2   BBC news website at http://news.bbc.co.uk/1/hi/uk/7641734.stm (accessed 30 September 2008)

3   www.conservatives.com/News/Articles/2006/04/Letwin_Why_we_have_signed _up_to_Labours_anti-poverty_target.aspx (accessed 30 September 2008)

4   Given the financial changes in recent times, it would be of great interest to be able to replicate our measures on the latest waves of data, but they are not yet available.

5   See for example, Calandrino, *Low Income and Deprivation in British Families*, DWP Working Paper 10, 2003; S Ringen, 'Direct and Indirect Measures of Poverty', *Journal of Social Policy* 17(3),1988, pp351-65

6   A Yeo, *Experience of Work and Job Retention Among Lone Parents: an evidence review*, DWP Working Paper 37, Corporate Document Services, 2007

7   P Morris, L Gennetian and G Duncan, *Effects of Welfare and Employment Policies on Young Children: new findings on policy experiments conducted in the early 1990s*, MDRC, 2005

Appendix

Calculating relative poverty rates using the Poverty Index

The traditional way of calculating relative poverty is to use some fraction of median (or mean) income as the cut-off point and then count everyone below this as 'poor'. With respect to the Poverty Index, there are problems with this approach.

In order to measure adequately relative poverty headcounts, it is necessary to have a fixed baseline below which no one can fall. With income measures this is straightforward as no one can have a negative income and so relative indicators based on a fraction of mean and median income then make sense. With the Poverty Index, there is no effective zero position, which leads to a second problem in that, unlike when using income, negative values for the Poverty Index are possible. Thus, calculating cut-offs based on the mean and median is no longer valid over time (although threshold values of the Poverty Index are still possible to calculate absolute poverty figures).

Thus, the Poverty Index needs to be 'normalised' before *relative* poverty headcounts can be calculated. The strategy adopted was to calculate a maximum value of the Poverty Index for the model PI_{max}. This is the highest score anyone can actually have (ie, with no income, no possessions, maximum stress, no social contact, no civic participation, maximum financial strain etc). The Poverty Index was then transformed into a normalised wellbeing index W:

$$W = (-PI) + PI_{max}$$

This essentially reverses the distribution and sets a minimum at zero. This effectively creates an index of wellbeing where a person who is as badly off as one can be will always have a score of zero (W=0). Everyone else will be measured relative to that hypothetical person. No one can have a negative score.

Relative poverty rates were then calculated based on median fractions of the mean of 'the 'wellbeing' index W. Means and medians of W gradually increase over time and the relative poverty rates slowly fall.

Model 1

Year	Mean W	Median W	Headcount (%) based on median (W) x		
			.8	.85	.9
1991	4.36	4.45	13.5	19.2	27.5
1993	4.40	4.48	12.6	18.3	26.8
1995	4.46	4.55	11.6	17.4	26.3
1997	4.53	4.65	11.5	17.2	26.1
1999	4.55	4.66	10.9	16.7	25.0
2001	4.59	4.70	10.2	15.4	23.8
2003	4.63	4.73	9.7	14.8	23.0